The Import Of Color Symbolism In Sir Gawain

And The Green Knight

Joseph F. Eagan

<u>Printing Statement:</u>

[Reprinted from *Saint Louis University Studies,* Series A, Vol. 1, November, 1949.]

THE IMPORT OF COLOR SYMBOLISM IN
SIR GAWAIN AND THE GREEN KNIGHT

By Joseph F. Eagan, S.J.*

It is the purpose of the first part of this study to discuss the existence of a fascinating medieval language of colors, in which the most commonly used colors had definite meanings attached to them.[1] Since this language of color symbolism is part of a larger symbolic habit of mind characteristic of the Middle Ages, it will be advisable first briefly to indicate the predominance of symbolism in all phases of medieval life before attempting to consider evidence for the meanings of individual colors.

PART I

Symbolism in Medieval Life

The Middle Ages are the golden age of symbolism. Wherever the medieval man went, whatever he did, he could not escape this universal, international language of symbolism. When he began the day with Mass in his great Gothic Cathedral, he went to the greatest medieval treasure-house of symbolism.[2] As he entered through the great arched doorway, he saw in the deeply recessed portals numerous sculptured figures of saints and Old Testament characters, each identified by its traditional symbol; within the mighty structure, brilliant stained-glass windows told him Old and New Testament stories, which he immediately recognized through the symbolic colors and objects traditionally assigned to each figure; and as he looked far up the nave, at the candle-lit altar, he saw a priest move through the richly symbolic liturgy of the Mass in his costly red or purple or green or white vestments, which symbolized the character of certain feast days or periods in the Church calendar.

---

* A. M., Saint Louis University, 1948.

[1] The second part of the present study will attempt to suggest how color in its unusually frequent occurrence in *Sir Gawain and the Green Knight* is used symbolically according to these medieval meanings and how this color symbolism gives clearer, richer, more unified, and more conclusive meaning to the poem.

[2] F. R. Webber, *Church Symbolism* (Cleveland: J. H. Jansen, 1938), p. 13: "Every detail had its meaning, whether it was wrought in stone, in wood, in painted glass, in beaten metal, in mural paintings, in rich tapestries or in sumptuous needlework. The Medieval artist and craftsman turned every church into a richly colored text book in Bible History."

After Mass, the medieval man might see a group of knights
ride past, with their shining armor and gay shields flashing in the early
sun. He would know their family history and achievements written in
the language of heraldry—the bright colors and the various symbolic
figures on the shields. He might pass by the shops of those queer
but influential characters, the alchemist and astrologer, and see
their elaborately symbolic metals and astrological tables. He would
know at once the magic properties of each precious stone and would
recognize the symbols of the seven planets and of the twelve signs of
the zodiac. At home his recreational reading would be taken from the
vast body of allegorical literature, like the *Roman de la Rose*; or from
the great Arthurian cycle, or the courtly French romances, so full of
symbolic flowers, clothes, and love conventions; or from the bourgeois
bestiaries, fabliaux, and *exempla.* In short, the medieval man thought,
and prayed, and recreated in the midst of symbolism.

Reasons for this predominance of symbolism are not hard to find.
With all his sins and inconsistencies, medieval man was essentially
religious. As one writer says,

...of no truth was the medieval mind more conscious than of St. Paul's
phrase: *Videmus nunc per speculum in aenigmate, tunc autem facie ad faciem.*
The Middle Ages never forgot that all things would be absurd, if their meaning were exhausted in their function and their place in the phenomenal world, if
by their essence they did not reach into a world beyond this.[3]

Medieval man never ceased trying to pierce the veil of the supernatural
and to express in concrete form the sublime spiritual mysteries of his
religion. His only available means of expressing the spiritual in the
material was, of course, through the symbol, some visible object which
would lead to knowledge of the invisible. The great cathedrals with
their magnificent stained-glass windows, their profusion of sculptured
figures, wood carving, and metal work, the vast body of medieval
miniature painting and of illuminated manuscripts; and the whole rich
expanse of church liturgy with its brilliant vestments, noble chant, and
intricate ceremonial remain as convincing testimony of the successful
language of medieval religious symbolism.[4]

---

[3] J. Huizinga, *The Waning of the Middle Ages* (London: Edward Arnold and
Company, 1937), p. 183.

[4] Regarding sculpture in the medieval cathedral, the authors state that the whole
cathedral "...was a graven book of religious history, practice and doctrine which even the
illiterate could read." See Jeremiah O'Sullivan and John F. Burns, *Medieval Europe*
(New York: Appleton-Century-Crofts, Inc., 1943), p. 341.

Such a wealth of symbolism found in religion naturally induced a symbolic habit of mind.

The habit of the Medieval mind of reading into every leaf, and animal, and bird, and inanimate object, and number and ecclesiastical vestment a mystical meaning, and using it to point some moral, either true or fanciful, is one of the characteristics of that age.[5]

This symbolic habit was, however, manifested not only in the service of religion but in all phases of life—in the elaborate knighting ceremony, in the artificial code of courtly love, in the false magic of the day, in songs and writing, to mention only a few. It is, accordingly, not at all strange to discover symbolism prevalent in a field which delighted the Middle Ages so much, that of color, and to find there an unwritten but fully developed code of symbolism.

Origins of the Medieval Code of Color Symbolism

A fact that strikes us immediately is the continuity that seems to exist between the color symbolism in the Middle Ages and the usage of ancient times. Portal, in *Des Couleurs Symboliques*, illustrates the ancient origin of color meanings with many examples of colors used symbolically in early Egyptian, Chinese, Indian, Persian, and Hebrew religious rites and indicates the continuity of this code up to and through the Middle Ages by showing that the medieval color meanings are the same as those of ancient times.

La langue des couleurs, intimement unie à la religion, passe dans l'Inde, en Chine, en Egypte, en Grèce, à Rome; elle reparaît dans le moyen-âge, et les vitraux des cathédrales gothiques trouvent leur explication dans les livres zends, les Vedas et les peintures des temples égyptiens.[6]

This stream of color symbolism flowing from ancient times down to the Renaissance has many sources, four of which we can easily distinguish. The first source is the ancient religious rites of India, Persia, China, and Egypt. The second is the Old Testament, where we learn from the visions of the prophets the symbolic colors associated with God and the Heavenly Jerusalem, and where we discover, in the inspired writings, God's explicit choice of the colors for vestments and other objects to be used in sacred worship. The third source is the classical

---

5 Webber, *op. cit.,* p. 17.

6 Frederic Portal, *Des Couleurs Symboliques* ... (Paris: Treuttel et Wurtz, 1857), p. 2. The windows of Chartres cathedral, where Indian deities, Brahma and Vischnou, appear in the same window with Jesus, provide an example of this continuity. Cf. *ibid.,* p. 272: "Ce vitrail, fort antérieur à la renaissance, prouve la communication des mythes orientaux à l'époque des croisades; il unit les symboles de l'initiation chrétienne à ceux de l'initiation indienne."

mythology of Greece and Rome, and the rich color symbolism with
which the gods and goddesses, and their shrines are represented. The
fourth source, which is, of course, found in the first three, is what we
may call the natural, psychological, and therefore perennial meanings
of color. Primitive men in their superstitious beliefs and their religious
rites attached obvious meanings to the most impressive aspects of nature
about them—to the sky, darkness, light, the seasons, fire, the sun, and
so forth.[7]

This ancient color symbolism was assimilated into the art of the early
Christian church. Christian artists kept the same color meanings but
applied them in their liturgy and in their art to symbolize lofty spiritual
mysteries and to represent Christ, the Blessed Virgin, and the Saints.
It was this larger and richer stream, the ancient color symbolism
mingled with the early Christian color usages, that flowed into the
Middle Ages and determined the color symbolism of its shields, its
stained glass, its precious stones, its extensive church liturgy, and its
literature.[8]

Evidence for the symbolic meanings of individual colors in the
Middle Ages will, accordingly, be drawn from these five products of
medieval culture: heraldry, stained-glass windows, precious stones,
church liturgy and vestments, and literature. But before these symbolic
meanings are studied, another feature of the language of color symbolism should be considered.

Three Rules of the Language of Color Symbolism

As every language has certain unwritten rules guiding its logic, so
the language of color symbolism has its unwritten rules drawn from
man's actual symbolic use of colors. The three following rules are the
most important.

First, for the most part, only simple colors are used. This rule flows
from the very nature of symbolism, since a symbol is a sign by which
we come to know something not directly present or expressed. Accord-

[7] M. Channing Linthicum, *Costume in the Drama of Shakespeare and his Contemporaries* (Oxford: Clarendon Press, 1936), p. 15: "Certain meanings had naturally
become associated with colors even in pre-Christian times: red with blood, and hence with
power; yellow with the sun, therefore with warmth and fruitfulness; green with spring,
youth, hopefulness; brown with autumn and despair; grey with winter and barrenness;
white with purity; black—the absence of color—with darkness, constancy, gloom, woe, death."

[8] Further evidence of the identity of color meanings in ancient and medieval times
is found in Birren's preface to his table of the symbolisms of the tinctures in medieval
heraldry. Faber Birren, *The Story of Color* (Westport, Connecticut: The Crimson Press,
1941), p. 92: "The symbolisms of these tinctures follow the traditions of ancient civiliza-
tions and the Bible."

ingly, the object symbolized will be more quickly and clearly recognized if the symbol itself is clear and well-defined. A color symbol should not, therefore, be composed of several tints, each of which carries its own symbolism. This rule was quite carefully observed in ancient art and literature, and for the most part in the Middle Ages, for we find that only such colors as red, white, black, green, yellow, blue, and purple were used commonly in a symbolic sense. This rule, for example, was observed with the greatest scrupulosity in the medieval art of heraldry. Birren explains the reason for this.

The immutable law is established that no great ideal can possibly be symbolized except by pure color. Pink, lavender, and buff have no place on flags and devices. Dilute a color and the virtue for which it stands is thereby besmirched.[9] Heraldry, therefore, admits only the following tinctures (undiluted colors) : or, argent, gules, azure, sable, vert, purpure.[10]

However, in the later Middle Ages this rule was relaxed with the introduction of tints, a practice which gives rise to the second rule, that of combination of colors. By this rule, tints reecived their meanings from the colors which composed them; that which dominates, gives the general meaning, that which is dominated, the modified meaning.[11] Another way to modify the symbolical meaning of one of the pure colors was to associate it with another color. For example, black, the symbol of evil and wickedness, when associated with other colors, gives them a signification contrary to their usual meaning. Thus red, which signified divine and exalted love, when associated with black will symbolize infernal love, egoism, hatred, and all the passions of degraded man.[12] And yellow, a color with a noble signification, when associated with black will symbolize treachery, and felony in general. Frequently, however, composed colors (gray, brown) receive a clear, defined symbolic meaning from association with some object or from historical events, and thus do not take their meanings from the colors that compose them. An example of these non-color associative meanings is found in the color gray; composed of black and white, gray came to signify penance and humility from its association with ashes and with the garments of monks.

---

[9] *Loc. cit.*

[10] John E. Cussans, *The Grammar of Heraldry* (London: Longmans, Green and Company, 1866), p. 11. Tenne (orange) and sanguine (murrey) are sometimes included, though they are very seldom, if ever, used in English heraldry.

[11] Portal, *op. cit.,* p. 32.

[12] *Ibid.,* p. 33.

The third rule is the rule of opposites, according to which a meaning directly opposed to its ordinary meaning is attributed to a color. In the color blue we have an example of this reversal of meaning.

... by a very curious transition, blue, instead of being the colour of faithful love, came to mean infidelity too, and next, besides the faithless wife, marked the dupe. In Holland the blue cloak designated an adulterous woman, in France the "côte bleue" denotes a cuckold. At last blue was the colour of fools in general.[13]

This transferred meaning may have come about by unfaithful men dressing in blue to appear faithful, thus leaving themselves open to the charge of hypocrisy.

Symbolism of Individual Colors

1. White

Traditionally, white is symbolic of innocence, purity, holiness.[14] Examples of this meaning for white in the medieval Church occur with monotonous frequency. In his essay, *On English Liturgical Colours*, Atchley quotes the sequences or color-rules from the Sarum Consuetudinary (c. 1210), from the Consuetudinaries of Salisbury Cathedral (c. 1220), of Lichfield Cathedral (c. 1240), of Lincoln Cathedral (c. 1260), and of St. Paul's Cathedral Church (second half of thirteenth century), from the Exeter diocese sequence by John Grandisson (c. 1337), from the Wells *Ordinale et Statuta* (1340), and from the Evesham handbook of color-usage (1377);[15] in all of these white is prescribed for feasts of Virgins and Confessors and for all feasts of the Blessed Virgin. Pope Innocent III in the last quarter of the twelfth century includes these same symbolic meanings for white in chapter sixty-four of his *De Sacro Altaris Mysterio* and adds others:

... the colour white is used on Festivals of Confessors and Virgins, on the Feast of the Purification, as an emblem of the Virginal Purity of the Mother of God, ... at Easter, on account of the Angels, the witnesses and Heralds of the Resurrection....[16]

Pugin summarizes the use of white in ecclesiastical costume in the Middle Ages:

---

[13] Huizinga, *op. cit.*, p. 250.

[14] F. Edward Hulme, *The History, Principles and Practice of Symbolism in Christian Art* (London: Swan Sonnenschein and Company, 1899), p. 16.

[15] In E. G. Cuthbert Atchley, "On English Liturgical Colours," *Essays on Ceremonial* (London: De La More Press, 1904), pp. 107-146, *passim*, there is a treatment of color rules and sequences found in churches and dioceses in thirteenth and fourteenth century England.

[16] A. Welby Pugin, *Glossary of Ecclesiastical Ornament and Costume* (2d edition enlarged and revised by Bernard Smith; London: Henry G. Bohn, 1846), p. 244.

White is the most joyous of the canonical colours; the emblem of innocence and purity; the vesture in which angels and the redeemed are represented as clad in Heaven; the favorite of the Church alike in mourning and rejoicing; of all her colours the most ancient and universal.[17]

The two most representative literary figures of the Middle Ages, Dante and Chaucer, used the same symbolic meanings for white. In the description of the Apocalyptic Vision, in the *Purgatorio* of his *Divina Commedia*, Dante makes white symbolize faith, and the sinlessness and spotlessness of the elect.[18] A study of color symbolism in Chaucer[19] indicates that this representative English poet of the Middle Ages used white in its traditional meanings of innocence and purity, of faith, of joy, and of triumph. "The red and white of the youthful Squire suggest his ardent nature and his joyfulness."[20] Again, "green, white and red are the colors of the Knight's Tale .... white for triumph and purity...."[21] In the Prioress' Tale, the great preponderance of white symbolizes the typical innocence and purity of the characters. Thus, it seems to be "part of the artistic perfection of the Prioress' story of the 'little clergeon' that the only colors used [white and red] should express the Christian symbolism of purity and martyrdom."[22] Finally, in the *Second Nun's Tale* the old man wears a white robe to represent absolute truth and holiness.[23]

Similar symbolic evidence is found in the field of precious stones and heraldry. Bailey gives the following meanings for the diamond: light, innocence, purity, life, joy, invulnerable constancy;[24] and for the pearl: rarity, value, precious reward of patience, self-sacrifice, purity, wisdom.[25] In heraldry, argent or white represents faith and purity.[26]

---

[17] *Ibid.*, p. 243.

[18] Edward Moore. *Studies in Dante* ("Third Series"; Oxford: Clarendon Press, 1903), p. 184: "... white is the recognized colour to symbolize faith; ... all the figures alike were clothed in white garments, partly as it is the colour in which the Saints are always represented in the Book of Revelation, and also as it symbolizes Faith ...."

[19] Genevieve Martin, "Color and Color Symbolism in Chaucer" (Unpublished Master's thesis, Saint Louis University, 1944), p. 118. Mrs. Martin concludes: "... Chaucer makes free use of symbolic color meanings, and that he follows with practically unvarying consistency the established and traditional code of color symbols."

[20] *Ibid.*, p. 68.

[21] *Ibid.*, p. 74.

[22] *Ibid.*, p. 89.

[23] *Ibid.*, p. 95.

[24] Henry Turner Bailey, *Symbolism for Artists, Creative and Appreciative* (Worcester, Massachusetts: The Davis Press, 1925), p. 90.

[25] *Ibid.*, p. 162.

[26] Birren, *op. cit.*, p. 92.

2. Black

Black or black mixed with other colors seems to have been the favorite medieval color for symbolizing the devil and, consequently, evil. Chambers states that "a black face was a feature in the medieval representation of devils. . . ."[27] Hulme echoes this statement:

Black was in the Middle Ages associated with witchcraft. It is naturally a type of darkness, and therefore the transition to moral darkness and dealing with familiar spirits is readily made; hence such incantations and invocations of diabolic power were naturally known as the black art.[28]

In one of the religious paintings of the Middle Ages, St. John the Baptist wears a black tunic which symbolizes those souls who are dead to divine light and for whom he is imploring the divine mercy. Below the precursor, is a soul of one damned, whose black hair symbolizes his depravity.[29] Some medieval manuscript illuminators also represented Christ draped in black while he was fighting against evil; and the Virgin Mary, as the symbol of the Christian Church fighting against the powers of darkness, often appears with a black face in the Byzantine paintings of the twelfth century.[30] Likewise, in some old illuminated manuscripts, Jesus wears a black robe in the temptation scene.[31] Finally, black mixed with another color, for example with red, which Portal calls *roux* (a red-black), appears frequently in windows and miniatures to symbolize the devil or Hell or evil.[32]

To wickedness, de Bles, in his work on the costumes of the saints in art, adds death and mourning as common medieval symbolic meanings of black.[33] In the field of Church liturgy, black vestments were seldom used before the sixteenth century,[34] although we find this statement in the "Innocentian" sequence: "Black vestments are worn at times of affliction, and of fasting for sins, and for the departed."[35] Here we see

---

[27] E. K. Chambers, *The Medieval Stage* (Oxford: The Clarendon Press, 1904), p. 214.

[28] Hulme, *op. cit.*, p. 29.

[29] Portal, *op. cit.*, p. 29.

[30] *Ibid.*, p. 174.

[31] Anna Jameson, *Sacred and Legendary Art* (London: Longmans, Green and Company, 1879), I, 43.

[32] Portal, *op. cit.*, p. 270.

[33] Arthur de Bles, *How to Distinguish the Saints in Art* (New York: Art Culture Publications, 1925), p. 31.

[34] Pugin, *op. cit.*, p. 44.

[35] Atchley, *op. cit.*, p. 94.

the traditional symbolism of black for death and fasting. In Chaucer's *Trolius and Criseyde*, black is employed in this sense.[36]

In the language of heraldry, likewise, black had such sombre connotations as grief and penitence.[37]

3. Red

Red was the emblem of the Passion of Our Lord and in England was the customary liturgical color during Passion Week.[38] Its general signification was the intensity of divine charity and of martyrdom.[39] Symbolizing blood shed for the love of Christ, it was prescribed for the feast of all martyrs, as a medieval catalogue of vestments for the Church feasts indicates:

On Christmas day, all white, except the second Mass. On St. Stephen's day, all red, on St. John the Evangelist's day, all azure and white. On Holy Innocents' Day, all red. On St. Thomas the Martyr's Day, all red.[40]

Marbodus, bishop of Rennes, in an eleventh century poem on the twelve stones in the *Vision of New Jerusalem*, indicates that the blood color of the sardius shows the honor of the suffering martyrs.[41] In a medieval stained-glass window an angel is summoning two dead men from a tomb; his red robe indicates the kingdom of heaven which is divine love.[42] Dante uses red in the *Paradiso* to symbolize the theological virtue of charity which in heaven becomes perfect love.[43] And in the Apocalyptic Vision in the *Purgatorio*, Dante crowns the seven figures representing the later books of the New Testament, with a "perfect thicket of roses and other red flowers so that 'at a little distance one might have sworn that their heads were all on fire' (11. 145-50). In this use of red, Dante clearly symbolizes the supreme Evangelical virtue of charity or Love."[44]

[36] Martin, *op. cit.*, p. 106: "Black is used as a symbol of widowhood in the first appearance of Criseyde, and again as a symbol of the death of parting when Criseyde is sent to the Greek camp. In the beginning of the Prologue to Book Two the black waves are obviously hopeless grief."

[37] Birren, *op. cit.*, p. 92.

[38] Pugin, *op. cit.*, p. 194.

[39] *Loc. cit.*

[40] Atchley, *op. cit.*, p. 130.

[41] *Ibid.*, p. 172.

[42] Portal, *op. cit.*, p. 283.

[43] H. D. Austin, "Heavenly Gold: A Study in the Use of Color in Dante," *PQ*, XII (1933), 51.

[44] Moore, *op. cit.*, p. 184. See *ibid.*, p. 185, where Moore explains the symbolism of the purple color of the four cardinal virtues in the following way: In Dante's time red predominated in the color purple and was thus "the foundation and chief ingredient"; the symbolism is, therefore, that "even in the Cardinal Virtues, Charity or Love must be the prevailing feature."

Red was also used symbolically in medieval art to represent the
devil and passionate evil. A stained-glass window in Chartres Cathedral
pictures the devil with a red face, and in another section of the same
window the devil who tempts Jesus has red skin.[45] In a medieval
anecdote recounted by Froissart, the master of Carouges accused a
Jacques de Gris in 1386 of having seduced his daughter and challenged
him to a duel. Portal explains that the name Karl le Rouge (Carouges
or Charles the Red) signified to the medieval audience blood and
vengeance.[46]

In heraldry gules or red symbolizes either ardor or blood and
consequently courage;[47] while, among precious stones, the ruby signifies
love and passion.[48]

Hardly any other color in Chaucer has more rich symbolical
meanings than red. He employs it in almost all its traditional medieval
meanings: ardent love, courage, sensualism, martyrdom, and war. The
Wife of Bath exulted in red, for "she had Mars rising, and the powerful
Mars takes authority in her life. . . ."[49] In keeping with her Mars-like
boldness her red face and scarlet hair "indicated her love of mastery,
her uninhibited amorousness, and her frank sensualism."[50] In the
Knight's Tale red is used for war, Mars, and love;[51] in the Prioress'
Tale[52] and the Second Nun's Tale[53] for martyrdom. In the House of
Fame Venus' garland of red and white roses symbolizes ardent and
chaste love;[54] and the Squire's red and white flowers suggest his ardent
nature and joyfulness.[55] Chaucer is ironic when he gives Sir Thopas red
as a predominant color, knowing full well that Thopas is anything but
the ardent, courageous knight;[56] he is likewise ironic when he puts a
red carbuncle, the traditional amulet to prevent bleeding, on the shield
of the "invulnerable flower" of knighthood.[57] Finally, "the red beard of
the Miller told Chaucer's readers that the Miller was a 'cocher, thefe,
and scold.' "[58] A red beard, or red hair and complexion, seems to have

---

[45] Portal, op. cit., p. 274.
[46] Ibid., p. 284.
[47] Birren, op. cit., p. 92.
[48] Bailey, op. cit., p. 176.
[49] Martin, op. cit., p. 79.
[50] Ibid., p. 69.
[51] Ibid., p. 74.
[52] Ibid., p. 89.
[53] Ibid., p. 95.
[54] Ibid., p. 99.
[55] Ibid., p. 68.
[56] Ibid., p. 91.
[57] Ibid., p. 120.
[58] Ibid., p. 69.

been undesirable in the Middle Ages. Linthicum quotes from Curry's *Middle English Ideal of Personal Beauty* to the effect that "...a red beard with a red face seemed to have excited suspicion," and concludes his own discussion of the subject with the remark that

...red hair and beard, especially with red complexion, were disliked or distrusted by some persons during the Middle ages, and retained something of that aversion during succeeding generations.[59]

4. Blue

Symbolically and aesthetically, the colour blue possessed immense significance in the Middle Ages. Technically it was important to paintings to have a fine blue to complement the brilliant, warm red of vermillion; but the medieval attitude toward the colour goes deeper than that. It is hard to say whether the rarity and costliness of fine blues in cloths and pigments had a share in the origin of the esteem and honour in which the colour was held; or whether blue was chosen for the Virgin's robes because blue garments were rare and precious in medieval Europe....[60]

It is significant that blue appears seventeen times in Chaucer or only 4 per cent of the number of times other colors appear. Only brown, purple, and gray appear less in his works.[61] Perhaps the esteem almost approaching reverence in which blue was held explains its rare appearance in medieval times and its use for the expression of very special meanings. Whatever the explanation for its rarity, blue carried the most exalted symbolism in the Middle Ages: heavenly contemplation and Divine truth; constancy, fidelity, and loyalty; honor, virtue, and hope. In his *Sphere for Gentry* Sylvanus Morgan gives some indication of its use:

Blue signifieth divine contemplation. In moral virtues it signifieth godliness of conversation, and is of the color of air, attributed to celestial persons, whose contemplations have been about divine things, which was the cause it was so mainly used about the garments of the high priests under the Jewish dispensation.[62]

Further evidence for the exalted symbolic use of blue may be found in Fulvio Pellegrino Morato's *Rimorio de tutte le cadenze di Dante e Petrarca* (1528). Morato is cited by Linthicum as an authority for the statement that "throughout the ages, turquoise [a brilliant blue] had been the symbol of contemplation and elevated thought."[63]

---

[59] M. Channing Linthicum, "Something Browner than Judas's," *PMLA*, XLVII (1932), 806.

[60] Daniel V. Thompson, *The Materials of Medieval Painting* (New Haven: Yale University Press, 1936), p. 127.

[61] Alice E. Pratt, *The Use of Color in the Verse of the English Romantic Poets* (Chicago: University of Chicago Press, 1898), pp. 104, 115.

[62] Pugin, *op. cit.*, p. 44.

[63] M. Channing Linthicum, *Costume in the Drama of Shakespeare and His Contemporaries* (Oxford: Clarendon Press, 1936), p. 19.

Blue, the passionless color of the vault of the heavens, is likewise a natural symbol of Divine Truth.

Sur les peintures du moyen-âge, la robe du Messie est bleue pendant les trois années de sa prédication de vérité et de sagesse.[64]

The windows of Chartres, again, provide an example of the symbolism of blue. In one section, the Indian deity, Vischnou, is draped in blue and red, colors which express the twofold baptism of the spirit and of fire, of truth and of love; in another section of the red-black (le tanné ou rouge-noir) color of Brahma

...est le symbole de l'homme venant au monde et circonvenu par l'esprit des ténèbres;...Jésus, apparaissant dans la partie la plus élevée de la verrière, montre quel est le but vers lequel doivent tendre les fidèles; sa robe bleue indique qu'il est le Dieu de vérité. ...[65]

Probably the most popular symbolism of blue was constancy and fidelity, usually in love. In his study of color symbolism in the Middle Ages, and especially in Germany, Gloth says that the predominant symbolic use of blue is for constancy and fidelity in love.[66] A few of his numerous examples from medieval German poems reveal a lover with a blue banner to show his fidelity, a lover with a crown of blue blossoms to show that he will seek no other love if his own beloved dies, Lady Constancy with a crown of sapphires and on another occasion blue garments; in another poem a poet who sees near the coast a ship with blue sails, boards the ship and finds the walls of the cabin covered with blue satin; a blue flower is called *mannertreu* (fidelity to the wife); in a folk-tale the blue flower, succory, is a faithful wife waiting for her husband's return.[67] Chaucer gives the same symbolic value to blue in *The Clerk's Tale:* "Walter gives Griselda jewels set in gold and azure for a wedding gift. The symbolism of the azure is eternal fidelity."[68] And the order of the cross of Christian Charity, created by Henry III was blue to suggest faithful service.[69]

Other meanings of blue are hope, honor, and virtue in general. Marbodus, in his eleventh century poem referred to above, has the

---

[64] Portal, *op. cit.,* p. 149.

[65] *Ibid.,* pp. 272-273.

[66] Walthur Gloth, "Das Spiel von den sieben Farben," in *Teutonia Urbeiten Zur Germanischen Philologie,* by Dr. Wm. Uhl (Konigsberg: Grafe & Unzer, 1902), pp. 68-69. The reasons Gloth gives for this symbolism are instructive. Blue, he says, as the color of complete absence of passion and the coldest color, is the symbol of calm, dispassionateness, and indifference. It betokens the virtues which are farthest removed from passion: loyalty, modesty, discretion, constancy.

[67] *Ibid.,* pp. 66-71, *passim.*

[68] Martin, *op. cit.,* p. 81.

[69] See Portal, *op. cit.,* p. 241.

following verse on the symbolism of blue:

> Sapphirus habet speciem coelesti throno similem,
> Designat Cor simplicium spe certa praestolantium,
> Quorum vita et moribus refulget et virtutibus.[70]

Innocent III, writing to King Richard I in 1198, states that the calmness of the sapphire signifies Hope.[71] Bailey lists under sapphire the meanings of hope, truth, and heavenly reward;[72] while the heraldic azure signifies piety and sincerity.[73]

5. Green

Green, the joyful color of spring, took most of its symbolic meanings from the yearly phenomenon of the rebirth of life in nature, with its freshness, joyfulness, and newness. Green thus came to symbolize rebirth or regeneration in eternal life, the hope of this rebirth and faith in its accomplishment, youth and love, and chastity and contemplation.

Hope of rebirth in eternal life is a meaning frequently given to green in medieval times. Portal says that "Les peintres chrétiens du moyen-âge représentaient la croix de couleur verte, symbole de régénération, de charité, et d'espérance";[74] he gives the example of the Order of Our Lady of Chardon, instituted by Louis II, duke of Bourbon, in 1370, whose emblem was the cross enamelled with green to suggest hope.[75] In a medieval painting depicting the Last Judgment, Christ is seated on the golden throne of the sun and clothed in a gray mantle lined with green. Green here suggests the hope of immortal life.[76] In his interesting observation on the "heavenly colors" in Dante, Austin notes that green, which occurs frequently in the early parts of the *Divina Commedia,* disappears entirely in the *Paradiso.* He concludes that green symbolizes the exclusively temporal virtue of hope, for in heaven hope reaches utter fruition and becomes a word that no longer has meaning.[77] Moore sees the same hope-symbolism in the Apocalyptic Vision in

---

[70] Atchley, *op. cit.,* p. 172. The quotation from Marbodus in translation reads: "The sapphire has an appearance like to the throne of heaven; it signifies the simple of heart clothed in assured hope, whose life is resplendent with both good deeds and virtues."

[71] Sir Wm. St. John Hope and E. G. Cuthbert F. Atchley, *An Introduction to English Liturgical Colours* (London: Society for Promoting Christian Knowledge, 1920), p. 20.

[72] Bailey, *op. cit.,* p. 178.

[73] Birren, *op. cit.,* p. 92.

[74] Portal, *op. cit.,* p. 210.

[75] *Ibid.,* p. 244.

[76] *Ibid.,* p. 282.

[77] Austin, *op. cit.,* p. 51.

the *Purgatorio:*

The four living creatures representing the Evangelists are crowned with green leaves, the colour of Hope. They represent "the bringing in of a better Hope" (1.93); and their main purpose is to make known to us "Christ, who is our hope."[78]

A similarly persistent meaning for green is faith. Marbodus, in the *Vision of New Jerusalem,* indicates that the jasper signifies the vigor of faith.

> Jaspis, colore viridi praefert virorem fidei,
> Quae in perfectis omnibus numquam marcescit penitus,
> Cujus forti praesidio resistitur diabolo.[79]

Chaucer uses green in the *Knight's Tale*[80] for springtime, chastity, and youth; in the *Legend of Good Women*[81] for youth, gaiety, and hope; and in the *Parliament of Fowls* green, as the key color of the poem, is the color of Venus and of Nature.[82] This association with Venus, the goddess of the spring and of generation, along with youth and especially fresh youthful love, gave to green the meaning of chastity which was one of its symbolic meanings in the Middle Ages.

Gloth states that in German literature of the fourteenth and fifteenth century, green first meant the time of the beginning, for it is the color of the year's beginning; then, the beginning of the life of love and its happiness and joy; and finally, simply the color of love and joy. However, according to Gloth, the particular meaning of green in almost all German color language is the beginning of love. In *Der Magd Krone (The Maiden's Crown)*, a legendary work of the fourteenth century, green signifies the beginning of a glowing love for Christ.[83]

Sicard, bishop of Cremona, in his *Mitrale,*[84] and Durandus in his middle-thirteenth century *Rationale Divinorum Officiorum,*[85] associate the color green with contemplation. Sylvanus Morgan in the *Sphere of Gentry* says that green

... signifieth of itself the bountifulness of God, and in moral virtues, mirth, youth, and gladness. The green field is the emblem of felicity and prosperity to perpetuity, and is the symbol of the Resurrection.[86]

---

[78] Moore, *op. cit.,* p. 184.

[79] Atchley, *op. cit.,* p. 172. The quotation from Marbodus in translation reads: "Jasper, with its green color represents the strength of faith, which never wholly fades in any of the elect and which offers mighty resistance to the devil."

[80] Martin, *op. cit.,* p. 74.

[81] *Ibid.,* p. 109.

[82] *Ibid.,* p. 103.

[83] Gloth, *op. cit.,* pp. 58-61, *passim.*

[84] Hope and Atchley, *op. cit.,* p. 20.

[85] Hulme, *op. cit.,* p. 24.

[86] See Pugin, *op. cit.,* p. 150.

As in the case of other colors, it is heraldic language that best summarizes the most common meanings of green—youth and hope.[87]

Before closing this discussion of green we must note one of its very important and prevalent symbolical meanings; green in the Middle Ages was traditionally a fairy color. In his remarks concerning the color of the Green Knight in *Sir Gawain and the Green Knight,* Professor Hulbert says that the real explanation for the obvious emphasis on green is that it is "a color worn by Other-World beings."[88] He gives many examples of other-world creatures and fairies dressed in green and lists the works of many authorities who state that green was a fairy color.[89] He quotes from *Thomas Rhymer* to substantiate his statement that "green is the fairy color in the Ballads":

> The meist of them [ghosts] was clad in green
> To show the death they had been in.[90]

Hulbert concludes, in regard to the color of the Green Knight, that

... from the examples given above, among which it will be noticed are instances of green as a color of clothing, complexion, and horses, it is certain that the use of green here indicates that the Knight is an Other-World creature.[91]

6. Gold or Yellow

This colour in Arms, blazed by the name of Or, which is as much as to say Aurum, which is Gold.... Such is the Worthiness of this Colour, which doth resemble it, that none ought to bear the same in arms but Emperors and Kings, and such as be of the Blood Royal. And as this Metal exceedeth all others in Value, Purity, and Fineness, so ought the Bearer... to endeavor to surpass all others in Prowess and Virtue.[92]

This enlightening quotation reveals the most common medieval meanings attributed to yellow, the color of gold: worth, value, perfection, purity, honor—in a word, integrity. In heraldry, therefore, Or signifies honor and loyalty, according to Birren,[93] and love, constancy, and wisdom, according to Portal.[94] In medieval symbolism, the precious stone chrysoprase (purple with specks of gold), also suggests the idea

---

[87] Don C. Allen, in "Symbolic Color in the Literature of the English Renaissance," *PQ*, XV (1936), says that green in England always meant infidelity. Mrs. Martin, *op. cit.*, pp. 86-87, admits that once in Chaucer's *Against Woman Unconstant* green signifies fickleness but correctly argues that one instance of a meaning is not sufficient evidence (against the overwhelming evidence for other meanings) to establish fickleness as a dominant meaning for green.

[88] J. R. Hulbert, "Sir Gawaine and the Green Knight," *MP*, XIII (1915), 456.

[89] *Ibid.*, p. 456, footnote 7.

[90] *Ibid.*, p. 456.

[91] *Loc. cit.*

[92] Hulme, *op. cit.*, p. 21.

[93] Birren, *op. cit.*, p. 92.

[94] Portal, *op. cit.*, p. 88.

of perfection usually associated with gold, because it meant perfect love. Austin confirms this meaning of gold. The point he makes is that the color of hope, green, "drops out of Dante's *Divine Comedy* exactly at the point where the *Paradiso* begins, while gold, clearly the color of Heavenly Perfection, succeeds in its place."[95] He explains that in heaven hope reaches complete fruition, and hence gold signifies perfection, attainment, and divinity. Austin further adds that gold has two meanings: first, original perfection and unsullied purity, as in the so-called Golden Ages of any national literature; and second, that

... ultimate perfection which is attained after imperfection; that culmination of growth, that consummation devoutly anticipated by which full ripeness is at last reached, after the green preliminary states of promise and of hope, maturing in the yellow fruit and the golden grain.[96]

From these examples it is clear that many of the meanings of yellow come from the qualities of gold. A person who wears gold will be successful in all tests of his virtue, for gold signifies not only integrity and virtue but is "fixed" and stainless, that is, it will not vacillate or be tarnished under test.[97] Again, from a study of the attributes of gold, Pugin arrives at many of its common symbolic meanings.

A metal surpassing all others in purity and fineness and constantly employed in all kinds of ecclesiastical ornament. It is a meet emblem of Brightness and Glory. It is used for the nimbi which surround the heads of saints; frequently it forms the ground on which sacred subjects are painted, the better to express the majesty of the mystery depicted, and as it was most properly employed in the sacred vessels and sanctuary of the Old Temple, so the Chalices and Tabernacles of the New Dispensation, and the shrines of the Saints, have been moulded of this precious metal; while in multiplied fibres, and mingled with silk and purple, it enriches the sacerdotal vestments and the hangings of the altar. Gold signifies purity, dignity, wisdom, and glory. Vestments of gold or cloth, or of a gold ground, are allowed to be worn on all festivals, without exception, in lieu of any particular colour, on account of their great richness and beauty.[98]

Confirmation of several of these meanings of gold is found in Chaucer and medieval painting. In the *Second Nun's Tale* "the gold robe meant spiritual power and triumph such as was usually expressed

---

[95] Austin, *op. cit.*, p. 51.

[96] *Ibid.*, p. 48.

[97] H. Flanders Dunbar, *Symbolism in Medieval Thought and its Consummation in the Divine Comedy* (New Haven: Yale University Press, 1929), p. 442, quotes from John E. Mercer, *Alchemy, its Science and Romance*: "Thus gold is without stain, fixed, glorious, and able to undergo all tests." This symbolism is of particular interest relative to the abundant use of gold in *Sir Gawain and the Green Knight*.

[98] Pugin, *op. cit.*, p. 149.

in the halo of a saint," and "the gold letters of the Book symbolize revealed wisdom."[99] In one of the stained-glass windows depicting St. John the Baptist and Christ, noted above, we saw that the gold of John's black tunic signified the divine light, and the gilded hair of the elect their participation in the glory of divine light.[100] Portal says, further, that St. Peter, the support of the Church and the guardian of holy doctrine, was represented by the miniaturists and illuminators of the Middle Ages with a gilded yellow robe, which signified the purity of the heavenly revelation coming from God, as the sun and its rays symbolize the revealed light.[101]

However exalted much of its symbolism was, even the yellow of gold has its degraded meanings. As Portal notes, although *jaune d'or* was the emblem of love, of constancy, and of wisdom in the Middle Ages, pale yellow indicated treachery.[102] In twelfth century France, the doors of traitors and criminals were marked with yellow; and the Jews had to wear yellow, as did Judas in medieval paintings, to symbolize their treachery in betraying the Savior.[103] Chaucer's Pardoner in the *Prologue* has colpons of pale hair to symbolize his treachery.[104] The seeming contradiction in such meanings may be explained by the degree of purity of the yellow. Thus to the Moors, *"le jaune doré signifiait sage et de bon conseil, et le jaune pâle trahison et déception."*[105] Gloth says that the Greek custom of associating yellow with prostitutes continued into the Middle Ages,[106] so that yellow came to mean adultery. By the time of the Renaissance yellow meant inconstancy, jealousy, and adultery.

7. Purple

Purple is a color found very seldom in English medieval literature. According to the color chart in Miss Pratt's study, purple occurs once in Gower, twice in Chaucer, and not at all in Langland.[107] The relatively rare use of purple cloth, except by the nobility, may be a

[99] Martin, *op. cit.*, pp. 94-95.

[100] Portal, *op. cit.*, p. 283.

[101] *Ibid.*, p. 81.

[102] *Ibid.*, p. 294.

[103] *Loc. cit.*

[104] Martin, *op. cit.*, p. 69.

[105] Portal, *op. cit.*, p. 88. Phrases in bold face are italicized by Portal.

[106] Gloth, *op. cit.*, p. 81. Greek prostitutes wore yellow wigs, dyed their hair with saffron, and wore yellow garments.

[107] Pratt, *op. cit.*, pp. 103-104.

reason for its comparably infrequent appearance in literature.[108] There is difficulty, too, at times in identifying the color because of the indefinite meaning of the word "purple" in the Middle Ages. Pugin indicates that red was "more or less red," that is, it inclined toward purple, crimson, and violet according to the country from which it came; thus Tyrian red was an intense purple.[109] Miss Pratt calls "purple" the "most uncertain of all hues used by English poets."[110]

Its significance, however, is not difficult to determine. It holds to two basic meanings in the Middle Ages: One is derived from classical antiquity, the other, from Christian liturgy.[111] "Purple vestments, being esteemed to have the most nobility, emperors and princes, from their very cradle were dressed in purple."[112] Heraldic language follows classical antiquity in this, as in all its significations, for *purpure* means royalty and rank.[113] "Ecclesiastically, purple and violet have borne an entirely different signification, being devoted, not to imperial pomp, but to penitence and fasting."[114] In Christian art violet and purple signified passionate sorrow, suffering, and martyrdom; and Mary Magdalene as a penitent was pictured in violet.[115] Portal says that Christian symbolism gave to Christ a purple robe during His Passion.[116]

Sometimes the meanings for purple are drawn from the meanings of its component colors. Thus violet may mean love of truth from red (love) and blue (truth), or perseverance in sacrifice from red (sacrifice) and blue (constancy).

8. Gray

The Middle Ages reveled in bright colors, but only the nobility were permitted to dress gaily. The peasants and the poorer classes wore somber colors,[117] generally grays and browns,[118] which the courtly

---

[108] A sumptuary law, 1463, quoted from Isobel D. Thornley, *England Under the Yorkists, 1460-1485* (London: Longmans, Green and Co., 1920), p. 230, reads: "And also that no person under the state of a lord ... wear any manner cloth of silk, being of the colour of purple; upon pain to forfeit ... xli."
[109] Pugin, *op. cit.*, p. 199.
[110] Pratt, *op. cit.*, p. 8.
[111] Changes in these basic meanings of purple begin to occur in the Renaissance and especially in love literature. See, e.g., Herbert A. Kenyon, "Color Symbolism in Early Spanish Ballads," *Romanic Review*, VI (1915), 328.
[112] Pugin, *op. cit.*, p. 199.
[113] Birren, *op. cit.*, p. 92.
[114] Hulme, *op. cit.*, p. 27.
[115] Martin, *op. cit.*, p. 60.
[116] Portal, *op. cit.*, p. 302.
[117] Gloth, *op. cit.*, p. 47.
[118] Karl Weinhold, *Die Deutschen Frauen in dem Mittelalter* (Wien: Carl Gerald's Sohn, 1897), p. 254.

class was careful to avoid in its dress. These sombre colors appear rarely in medieval painting[119] and literature. Miss Pratt notes that brown fails to occur in Langland and Gower and appears only nine times in Chaucer (representing only 2 per cent of his total color usage), while grays appear three times in Langland, four times in Gower, and fifteen times (representing only 4 per cent of his total color usage) in Chaucer.[120]

Three meanings seem to predominate for gray in the Middle Ages: One is associated with the Last Judgment; another with penance and humility; and the third, a peculiar meaning, innocence accused. Portal says that miniatures of the fourteenth and fifteenth centuries representing the Last Judgment give Christ a gray mantle while He judges mankind, and the conclusion is that gray signifies the resurrection of the dead or, more particularly, of the flesh on the last day.[121] Portal explains also that the mixture of white and black (gray) was in Christianity the emblem of terrestrial death and of spiritual immortality.[122]

The association of penance and humility with gray probably comes from the color of ashes, the traditional Old Testament emblem of penance and abasement of self, and from the dress of the humble friars of St. Francis, the Franciscans or Gray Friars.[123]

One meaning of gray, which seems to have been quite common, is innocence accused or calumniated. Portal suggests that the origin of this symbolism is in the component parts of gray: white is innocence, black is culpability; united, they symbolize *innocence calomnieé, naircie.*[124] He further illustrates this meaning with the anecdote, narrated by Froissart, in which the master of Carouges accused Jacques de Gris of having seduced his daughter. Gris had promised to help Carouges in one of his expeditions and had fought valiantly. Did he violate his promise? Had he been disloyal to the daughter? The medieval man immediately recognized Jacques' total innocence, for in his familiar language of symbolism, Carouges or Karl le Rouge (red), as already noted, signifies blood and vengeance, while Gris (gray) indicates innocence accused.[125]

[119] Thompson, *op. cit.*, p. 88.
[120] Pratt, *op. cit.*, pp. 103-104.
[121] Portal, *op. cit.*, p. 281.
[122] *Loc. cit.*
[123] Jameson, *op. cit.*, p. 42. Their habit has since been changed to a dark rusty brown.
[124] Portal, *op. cit.*, p. 284.
[125] *Ibid.*, pp. 284-285.

9. Brown

Even more than gray, brown seems to have been the color of the peasants and the lowly. Being the color of the earth, it was readily associated with the serf. It became the sign of penance and humility when noblemen, wishing to do penance and to humiliate themselves, would throw off their brilliant court dress and don the sombre "weeds" of the peasant.[126] And it was the color of many of the habits of penitential religious orders, adopted as the symbol of renunciation of the world and of the combat against the powers of Hell.[127]

This relation of brown to asceticism suggests another very common meaning of the color in the Middle Ages. In his chapter on *Du Tanné* (tan or brown), Portal indicates one origin of the medieval symbolism involved.

La symbolique chrétienne reproduisit les différentes significations attachées à la couleur tannée par l'antiquité. Le dragon roux [reddish black or brown] de l'Apocalypse et le feu de l'enfer, dont parlent les évangiles, indiquent dans quel sens on doit interpréter le rouge-noir employé sur les vitraux et les miniatures du moyen-âge. La cathédral de Chartres offre ici un exemple. ...[128]

It is from this meaning of brown in the Bible that we learn to interpret certain browns of medieval paintings as symbolic of the devil and the powers of evil.[129] Thus, too, from the windows of Chartres cathedral, it appears that all the characters who in any way are related to evil— the devil, the personification of evil; St. Peter, who denied Jesus; Judas, who betrayed Him; and Jesus Himself, Who came into this world of evil to redeem mankind and who was tempted by Satan—all are clothed in brown (bistre or roux).

La cathédrale de Chartres offre l'emploi fréquent du *brun-rouge ou bistre* avec cette acception; sur la première ogive de la nef latérale du choeur, à droite, on voit une sainte cène; à gauche du Christ, deux personnages, vêtus d'un costume *bistre ou tanné*, semblent se disputer, Jésus les désigne de la main; ne serait-ce

---

[126] Curiously enough, when used as an adjective before a term signifying a weapon of war, especially the sword, brown seems to have been a conventional epithet meaning burnished or glistening. *NED* gives two examples of this meaning, one from about the year 1325, the other about 1380.

> Brende golde bry3t,
> As glemande glas burnist broun.
> > *EE. Allit. P.A.* 1. 989.
> Wyp ys swerd of style broun.
> > *Sir Ferumb.* 1. 5609.

[127] Portal, *op. cit.*, p. 277.

[128] *Ibid.*, p. 270.

[129] *Ibid.*, p. 277: "La couleur tannée ou brune était encore, dans l'antiquité et le moyen-âge, un signe de deuil. Les Juifs portaient des cilices noirs ou bruns. Sur les anciennes peintures qui représentent la passion du Christ, on voit souvent des personnages vêtus de robes brunes."

pas Judas qui trahit son maître et Pierre qui le renia. La tradition donne des *cheveux roux* à Judas.

Au bas de cette scène paraît le diable, sa peau est bistre, son museau est rouge. ...A droite, Jésus est tenté, il parte *un manteau bistre*; ...A gauche de ce sujet, un autre vitrail représente de même la tentation de Jésus; il est encore vêtu d'un *manteau bistre*; ...

Dans la partie supérieure de cette ogive, paraît la Vierge drapée de bleu; sur ses genoux repose l'enfant Jésus vêtu de *bistre*. Cette couleur marque ici que l'enfant divin naquit dans le péché comme les autres autres hommes, et pour les sauver s'associa à toutes leurs misères.[130]

In another window at Chartres, Brahma in brown represents the man who comes to the world and is led astray by the spirit of darkness: "Sa couleur est celle de l'enfer, le tanné ou rouge-noir."[131] The same window shows Jesus in brown as the savior who came to overcome evil: "le manteau bistre du Seigneur témoigne qu'il est descendu sur cette terre pour vaincre l'esprit du mal."[132]

The following outlines are an attempt, first, to summarize the various symbolic meanings for each color by showing the probable logical evolution of such meanings; and, second, to list with some completeness the various standard color meanings prevalent especially in ancient and medieval times and to some extent in modern times. The outlines indicate, first, the basic origin of the symbolism and, second, the logical extensions of meanings flowing from this basic origin. These various meanings are drawn from all the sources used in this study, as well as from eleven summaries of color meanings given by scholars in their works on color, on painting, or on the middle ages in general.[133]

---

130 *Ibid.*, pp. 274-275. The italics are inserted.

131 *Ibid.*, p. 272.

132 *Ibid.*, p. 273.

133 See, e.g.: Henry Turner Bailey, *Symbolism for Artists, Creative and Apprecia-tive;* Faber Birren, *The Story of Color,* pp. 103-106; Arthur de Bles, *How to Distinguish the Saints in Art by their Costumes, Symbols, and Attributes,* pp. 30-33; Clara Erskine Clement, *A Handbook of Legendary and Mythological Art,* pp. 7-8; Ellen Conroy, *The Symbolism of Color;* F. Edward Hulme, *The History, Principles, and Practice of Sym-bolism in Christian Art,* pp. 16-29; Anna Jameson, *Sacred and Legendary Art,* pp. 41-43; Mrs. Henry Jenner, *Christian Symbolism,* pp. 165-167; M. Luckiesh, *The Language of Color,* pp. 100-139; Thomas O'Hagan, *The Genesis of Christian Art,* pp. 40-41; A. E. H. Swaen, *Englishe Studien,* "An Essay in Blue," LXXI (1936-1937), 1-15; "Greenery Gallery," LXXII (1937-1938), 343-354; "The Palette Set," LXXIV (1940), 62-88.

The supposition on which these outlines have been constructed is that primitive man naturally associated certain meanings with certain colors. The religious and cultural folklore of ancient peoples testify that he drew color meanings from objects most immediate to his experience, that is, himself and his fellow man, nature, and the things he used. Thus red became associated with blood and then with war, yellow with the sun and therefore with warmth and fruitfulness, green with spring and therefore with youth and hopefulness, and so forth. From these primitive meanings, by association and extension of meanings, there was built up a rich symbolism of colors.

To simplify the outlines, only the predominant meanings have been given—for example, the virtues of faith for white, or of hope for green, although blue sometimes signifies both hope and faith. Further, meanings have not been included that were occasioned by certain historical events and that were formulated according to the rule of opposites—for example, blue as signifying infidelity and cuckoldry, yellow as signifying treachery and adultery, because these meanings did not "evolve" by a natural association.

White

Purity, chastity, virginity
Peace, joy, happiness
Holiness of life, innocence
The elect in heaven, saints
Triumph, victory
Faith
God, Eternal Light and Truth
Candor, honesty
Knowledge, goodness, truth

Red

Anger, hate, war, cruelty, suffering
Love, charity
Sin, adultery, passion
Courage, zeal
Patriotism, anarchism
Sacrifice, martyrdom
Shame, laughter, enthusiasm
Hell
Royalty
Life, health

Green

Generation, fertility, abundance
Chastity
New life, Eternal Life, Immortality,
  hope of eternal life
Victory
Joy, contentment, contemplation
The preternatural
Youth, immature, vigorous, love,
  hope, confidence

Brown

Death, sadness
Quietness
Maturity
Laboring man, the humble, poverty

Humility, penance, renunciation,
  monasticism
Satan, Hell, evil, suspicion

Black

Evil, devil, witchcraft
Ignorance, error
Death, mourning
Sleep, slience
Negation, privation
Solemnity, profundity

Blue

Heaven, divinity, eternity
Intelligence, truth, contemplation,
  reason, Justice
Self-control, fidelity, loyalty, honor
Serenity, constancy, contemplation,
  wisdom
Sincerity, truth

Yellow or Gold

Fruitfulness, marriage, love
Maturity, mellowness
Wisdom
God, His wisdom, bounty
Power, strength
Glory
Cheerfulness, joy
Integrity, goodness, honor
Value, dignity

Gray

Penance, humility, mourning
Monasticism
Barrenness, sadness, dreariness
Innocence accused
Old age, retrospection, ripened
  judgment

Purple

Suffering, endurance, penance, Lent
Royalty, dignity, splendor
Love of truth, honor
Mourning

White

I. Unstained, unspotted, unadulterated
- purity—moral order { chastity—virginity / innocence—peace—joy, happiness }
- holiness, moral perfection
- the Elect in heaven
- unity

II. Light
- its daily triumph over darkness { triumph, victory—Faith / Truth }
- contrasted to darkness { Prince of Darkness vs. Uncreated Light / Eternal Light—divinity, God / Eternal Truth vs. Prince of error }
- its clarity—candor, honesty

III. Opposition to Black
- ignorance—knowledge
- evil—good
- sorrow—joy
- secret—candor
- devil—God
- error—truth
- folly—wisdom

SUM: Basic Derivation—1. Unstained Quality
2. Light—its attributes
—eternal duality, fight between light and darkness

Black

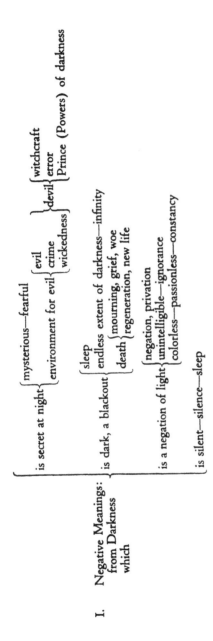

I. Negative Meanings: from Darkness which

- is secret at night {
  mysterious—fearful
  environment for evil { evil / crime / wickedness } devil { witchcraft / error / Prince (Powers) } of darkness

- is dark, a blackout {
  sleep
  endless extent of darkness—infinity
  death { mourning, grief, woe / regeneration, new life }

- is a negation of light {
  negation, privation
  unintelligible—ignorance
  colorless—passionless—constancy

- is silent—silence—sleep

Combination of these 4 attributes—solemnity, profundity

II. Positive Meaning {
  solid basic or structural strength
  constancy (colorless, passionless)

SUM: Basic Derivation—1. Night and Darkness
2. Opposition to light and to white

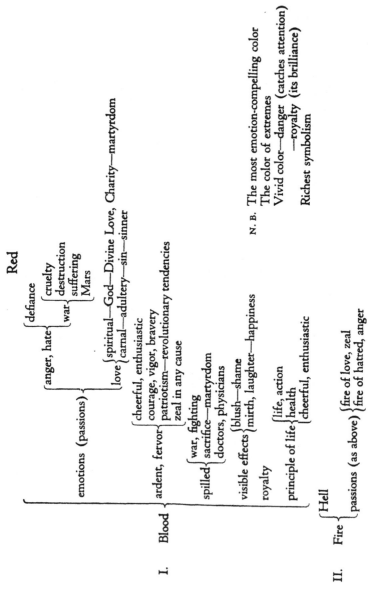

Red

I. Blood

- emotions (passions)
  - anger, hate { defiance; war { cruelty, destruction, suffering, Mars
  - love { spiritual—God—Divine Love, Charity—martyrdom; carnal—adultery—sin—sinner
- ardent, fervor { cheerful, enthusiastic; courage, vigor, bravery; patriotism—revolutionary tendencies; zeal in any cause
- spilled { war, fighting; sacrifice—martyrdom; doctors, physicians
- visible effects { blush—shame; mirth, laughter—happiness
- royalty
- principle of life { life, action; health; cheerful, enthusiastic

II. Fire { Hell; passions (as above) { fire of love, zeal; fire of hatred, anger

SUM: Basic Derivations—1. Blood 2. Fire

N. B. The most emotion-compelling color
The color of extremes
Vivid color—danger (catches attention)
—royalty (its brilliance)
Richest symbolism

Blue

Sky or Heavens {

the firmament, heaven—Divinity, gods {
- Supreme Intelligence
- Truth (Heavenly, divine truth)
- contemplation
- heavenly love—love of divine works { piety, justice
- eternity—human immortality

air—breath, spirit—spiritual qualities in man

- is cool—passionless {
  - self-control { chastity, fidelity, loyalty
  - reason, intelligence { prudence, justice
  - dignified, soothing

Sky—
- is quiet when pure blue—serenity, tranquility, calmness {
  - constancy, fidelity
  - contemplation { wisdom, truth

- is clear—sincerity—truth

}

SUM: Basic Derivation—Sky { heavens, attributes of sky

Green

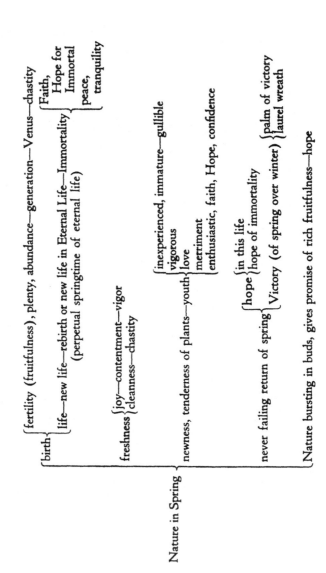

```
        ┌ fertility (fruitfulness), plenty, abundance—generation—Venus—chastity
        │
        │                                                            ┌ Faith,
birth ⎨  life—new life—rebirth or new life in Eternal Life—Immortality ⎨ Hope for
        │                 (perpetual springtime of eternal life)       │ Immortal
        └                                                              ⎩ peace,
                                                                         tranquility

            ⎧ joy—contentment—vigor
freshness ⎨
            ⎩ cleanness—chastity

                                                ┌ inexperienced, immature—gullible
                                                │ vigorous
newness, tenderness of plants—youth ⎨  love
                                                │ merriment
                                                └ enthusiastic, faith, Hope, confidence

                                      ⎧ hope ⎨ in this life
never failing return of spring ⎨            ⎩ hope of immortality
                                      ⎩ Victory (of spring over winter) ⎨ palm of victory
                                                                          ⎩ laurel wreath

Nature bursting in buds, gives promise of rich fruitfulness—hope
```

Nature in Spring

SUM: Basic Derivation—Nature at Spring—its attributes

Gold or Yellow

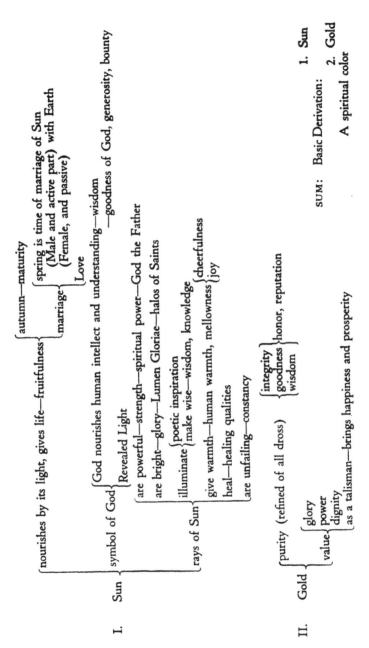

I. Sun

— nourishes by its light, gives life—fruitfulness
  — autumn—maturity
  — spring is time of marriage of Sun
    (Male and active part) with Earth
    (Female, and passive)
  — marriage
    — Love

— symbol of God
  — God nourishes human intellect and understanding—wisdom
    —goodness of God, generosity, bounty
  — Revealed Light—God the Father

— rays of Sun
  — are powerful—strength—spiritual power
  — are bright—glory—Lumen Gloriae—halos of Saints
  — illuminate { poetic inspiration
                 make wise—wisdom, knowledge
  — give warmth—human warmth, mellowness { cheerfulness
                                            joy
  — heal—healing qualities
  — are unfailing—constancy

II. Gold

— purity (refined of all dross) { integrity
                                   goodness } honor, reputation
                                   wisdom

— value { glory
          power
          dignity

— as a talisman—brings happiness and prosperity

SUM: Basic Derivation: 1. Sun
                         2. Gold

     A spiritual color

Gray

I. Color of ashes—penance $\left\{\begin{array}{l}\text{humility}\\ \text{mourning}\\ \text{tribulation}\end{array}\right\}$ monasticism

II. Leaden skies, winter, rainy days—dreariness, depression, barrenness, sadness, gloom, grief

III. Gray hair of old age $\left\{\begin{array}{l}\text{the past—retrospection}\\ \text{maturity—ripened judgment—discretion}\end{array}\right.$

IV. Gray $\left\{\begin{array}{l}\text{white==innocence}\\ \text{black==sin}\end{array}\right.$ —innocence besmirched, innocence accused, faith not believed

$\left\{\begin{array}{l}\text{white==enlivening}\\ \text{black==gloomy}\end{array}\right.$ —gentle sadness, melancholy

Purple

I. High cost of purple dye in antiquity—royalty {honor
splendor, dignity {imperial Rome—color of state
—mourning
purple composed of warm and cool colors, is a soothing color—soothing, calming

II. Christ wore purple during Passion—suffering—endurance—penance and mortification {Lent
repentance—sorrow

III. Purple {red—love, sacrifice
blue—truth} love of the truth, wisdom, honor

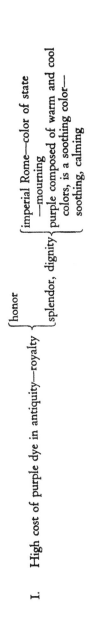

Brown

I. Color of autumn
$$\begin{cases} \text{decay—death—sadness} \\ \text{life softly passing away—quietness, softness} \\ \text{maturity} \end{cases}$$

II. Color of earth
$$\begin{cases} \text{earthy—laboring man, peasant} \begin{cases} \text{poverty} \\ \text{the humble} \begin{cases} \text{humility} \\ \text{penance} \end{cases} \end{cases} \\ \text{strength—solidity, vigor} \end{cases}$$

III. Medieval color of the peasants, humble folk—the humble—humility—penance—renunciation of world—monasticism

IV. Brown $\begin{cases} \text{red—Hell fire} \\ \text{black—darkness} \end{cases}$ Satan, livery of Hell—Evil—love of darkness—suspicion

PART II

COLOR SYMBOLISM IN

Sir Gawain and the Green Knight

In Part I of this study the widespread use of color symbolism in the Middle Ages was considered. In Part II an attempt will be made to show, first, that the author of *Sir Gawain and the Green Knight* employs colors in their medieval symbolic meanings and, second, that these meanings shed some light on a possible new interpretation of the poem. But before any symbolic use of colors is discussed, the theme or basic meaning of the poem will have to be determined.

The theme of any literary work is its basic meaning. Since every work of art is somehow an expression of a man's own self—of his likes and dislikes, and of his philosophy of life—the basic meaning of a particular piece of literature will be an expression of the writer's personal attitude toward this particular subject matter. Because his attitude toward a definite phase of life moves the writer to express himself, the theme also represents his intention in writing.

In *Sir Gawain and the Green Knight,* the subject matter is Sir Gawain and his adventures, and the theme is the significance which the Gawain-poet attaches to them. He has revealed his own feelings and attitudes toward Gawain and his deeds and has thus evidenced his intention in composing the poem. By careful study of such evidence we should be able to arrive at the basic meaning of the poem. Frequently, however, skillful artists will have two levels of meaning: one, more obvious, which is easily gathered from explicit statements and actions in the poem; the other, more subtle and hidden, which is detected only by careful study of conversation and by weighing statement against statement, incident against incident. Often this more subtle meaning turns out to be satirical.

An attempt will be made to analyze carefully the text of *Sir Gawain,* but no study will be made of the origins of plot, character, and episode in preceding romances and folklore myths. The study of origins has been the chief point of interest on the part of almost every scholar in the past half-century who has written on *Sir Gawain and the Green Knight*; such scholars as Weston, Kittredge, Hulbert, and others have devoted much research to the origins of the poem and have, in many instances, determined probable sources which have suggested some interpretations. The prime interest here, however, is with the actual poem itself as we now have it; the findings and conclusions of these scholars on its origins are of concern to us only in so far as they help to interpret the poem.[1]

Since no analysis of a narrative poem can be made intelligible without a clear knowledge of the facts of the story, a brief resumé of the essential facts of the Gawain story follow.

The Story

Part 1 (ll. 1-490)

On New Year's day King Arthur sits with his knights at a great feast in Camelot. According to his custom, he will not begin the feast before he has heard some marvelous adventure. Suddenly a huge knight, dressed entirely in green, with green skin and hair, rides into the great hall brandishing an immense battle-axe; he dismounts from his green horse and challenges the court to a Christmas game, inviting one of Arthur's knights to strike him a blow with the axe, on the condition that a year later the Green Knight shall return the blow. The whole court is silent. When the Green Knight taunts the court for its cowardice, Arthur blushes for shame and rises to answer the challenge; but Gawain courteously asks and receives permission from his lord to undertake the adventure in his place. Gawain promises to seek the Green Knight a year later at his abode and with one stroke sends the green head rolling on the floor. The knight retrieves it immediately and holds it up with his hand; from this position the head reminds Gawain to meet the Knight next New Year's day at the "Green Chapel." The Green Knight rides wildly from the hall.

---

[1] There is, accordingly, no concern here with the controversy whether or not the Gawain poet took his tale from a lost French original which first combined the Challenge and Temptation plots (Kittredge); whether the Green Knight was originally a vegetation God (Nitze) or an Irish Sun God (Buchanan) or the Lord of Hades (Krappe); whether or not Bercilak was a personal acquaintance of the Gawain-poet (Wright); whether the original motive of the Beheading was disenchantment (Kittredge) or the original story the luring of Gawain by an other-world fee who loved but had never seen him (Hulbert); or finally, whether or not Morgan le Fay was added merely to give the poem an Arthurian setting (Kittredge). For an exposition of these views consult the following references: J. L. Kittredge, *A Study of Gawain and the Green Knight* (Cambridge, Mass.: Harvard University Press, 1926). (Fraulein von Schaubert in *Englische Studien*, XVII, has postulated an immediate English origin, rather than a French one.) W. A. Nitze, "Is the Green Knight Story a Vegetation Myth?" *MP*, XXXIII (1936), 351-366; Alice Buchanan, "The Irish Framework of *Gawain and the Green Knight*," *PMLA*, XLVII (1932), 315-338; A. H. Krappe, "Who Was the Green Knight?" *Speculum*, XIII (1938), 215; Elizabeth M. Wright, "Sir Gawain and the Green Knight," *JEGP*, XXXIV (1935), 157-159; Kittredge, *op. cit.*, pp. 117-118; J. R. Hulbert, "Sir Gawain and the Green Knight," *MP*, XIII (1915), 459; Kittredge, *op. cit.*, pp. 132-133 and Hulbert, *op. cit.*, p. 454.

Part 2 (ll. 491-1125)

The year passes swiftly through the seasons, and finally on All Souls day, amid the weeping of the court, Gawain sets out for the Green Chapel. After suffering intensely from cold and from storms, and after conquering many giants and wild beasts, he finds himself in a deep forest on Christmas Eve. He prays devoutly to Mary for a lodging in which to hear the Mass of Christ's birth and immediately sees a shining white castle. He is there given lodging and is nobly entertained until the feast of St. John by the merry Lord and his fair wife (whom Gawain considers more beautiful even than Guenever), by the ladies of the Castle, and by an ancient and ugly dame, the companion of the Lord's wife. When he learns that the Green Chapel is only two miles away, Gawain accepts the Lord's urgent invitation to remain with him until New Year's day. Before retiring, the Lord proposes a merry bargain to which Gawain agrees: On each of three successive days Gawain shall sleep late and spend the day with the Lord's wife, while the Lord himself goes hunting; at night each shall give the other what he had gained during the day.

Part 3 (ll. 1126-1997)

Each morning the Lord sets out very early for the chase; and each morning his fair wife steals into Gawain's bedroom, sits beside him, very frankly offers herself to him, and converses at great length about the joys and sorrows of love-making. Gawain is sorely tempted but by his courtesy and artful speech parries her advances. The first day he receives one kiss, the second two, and the third three; each night he faithfully returns the kisses to the Lord, and receives in turn the spoils of a deer-hunt, a boar-hunt, and a fox-hunt. On the third day the Lady offers him a ring as a token of her love. He refuses the ring but accepts a magic girdle which she promises will preserve its wearer from wounds and death. Gawain breaks his compact by concealing the girdle from the Lord.

Part 4 (ll. 1998-2530)

On New Year's morning a servant of the Lord conducts Gawain toward the Chapel, tempting him to turn back by a recital of the horrible deeds of the Green Knight. Gawain impatiently rejects the suggestion and, entrusting himself to God, rides on alone through rough woods to a fearful cave in a green mound—the Green Chapel. Despite the horrible sound of an axe being sharpened on a grindstone, Gawain calls out loudly to the master of the place. The Green Knight appears,

leaps over the stream, and greets Gawain. True to his word, Gawain
bares his neck, but flinches at the first blow and is reproached for
cowardice. The Green Knight checks the second blow and only slightly
wounds Gawain with the third. The Knight then reveals himself as
Bercilak de Hautdesert. He praises Gawain as the most valiant of
knights and explains that the ancient dame, Morgan le Fay, had sent
him to test Arthur's court, and that he, in turn, had allowed his wife to
test Gawain. Gawain has suffered a slight wound on the third blow,
because on the third day he had concealed his winning of the girdle.
Shamed, Gawain curses his cowardice and covetousness and flings the
girdle at the Knight; but, when urged to keep it, he accepts the girdle as
a sign of his shame and returns to Arthur's court. After he has
recounted his adventures, the entire court agrees to wear a girdle as a
baldric to honor its victorious hero.

Structural Elements of the Story

In its barest structural elements, the story is composed of the
Challenge or Beheading Test and the Temptation or Wooing Test.
These plot elements are joined in the poem by the Lord's compact to
exchange the daily winnings. Thus, as Gawain learns at the Green
Chapel, his preservation in the Beheading Test was a consequence of
his victory in the Temptation Test. The mutual agreement to exchange
the daily winnings has an important further significance in the poem—
it binds in close parallel the three hunting scenes to the three temptation scenes.[2] (This parallel will be discussed at length later in this study.)

Dependent on these three structural elements (the Challenge, the
Temptation, and the Exchange of Winnings) are the various tests of
the poem: first, the courage of Arthur's court in accepting the Green
Knight's challenge; second, Gawain's courage and fidelity to his word in
seeking the Green Knight; third, Gawain's courtesy in the obedience of
a guest to his host; fourth, his chastity in the Temptation; fifth, his
fidelity to his word in the exchange of winnings; sixth, his honesty and
courage in refusing the servant's plea to turn back and say that he
could not find the Green Knight, and his courage in baring his neck to
the axe; and, finally, throughout the poem, the genuineness of his piety
and devotion to God and Mary. These various tests are the best clues

---

[2] Henry L. Savage, "The Significance of the Hunting Scenes in *Sir Gawain and
the Green Knight,*" *JEGP*, XXVII (1928), 1-15.

to the basic meaning of the poem and must, in turn, form the basis of this analysis and interpretation.

As was mentioned above, a poem often has two levels of meaning; and consequently, its theme can be expressed only by stating both these meanings. Such is the case with *Sir Gawain and the Green Knight*. The first level of meaning is the literal meaning. It is a test of the court of Arthur, in the person of its most illustrious knight, for all its knightly qualities, but especially for its chastity. The second level of meaning is the Gawain-poet's satirical intention. He wishes to satirize contemporary romances both for their glorification of the code of courtly love in its threefold aspect—its adultery, its deification of women, its absurd sentimentality and artificiality—and for their glorification of a degenerate chivalry. The following evidence from the poem itself would seem to warrant these two meanings.

First Level of Meaning

A Test of the Court of Arthur

The strongest evidence that the whole court of Arthur is being tested is found in Bercilak's words to Gawain at the Green Chapel (ll. 2456-58). He tells him that Morgan le Fay had sent him in the form of the Green Knight to test the pride of the Round Table and to see if its current great fame is deserved. Again the entire court, knight and lady, wears a green girdle as a baldric when Gawain returns from his adventures, to signify both his victory and his shame (ll. 2513-21). The fact that the court thus identifies itself with Gawain's victory and defeat indicates that it too was tested and found both victorious and defective. Finally, the Green Knight ridicules the entire court because it does not accept his challenge; he taunts it with its widespread fame, its fierceness, its pride and its past conquests.

'What, is þis Arþures hous,' quoþ þe haþel þenne,
'þat al þe rous rennes of þurȝ ryalmes so mony?
Your gry[n]de-layk & your greme & your grete wordes?
Now is þe reuel & þe renoun of þe Rounde Table
Ouer-walt wyth a worde of on wyȝes speche;
For al dares for drede, with-oute dynt schewed!' (ll. 309-15) [3]

[3] The text used in this study and the one from which all quotations have been taken is that edited by Israel Gollancz, *Sir Gawain and the Green Knight* ("Early English Text Society," O.S. no. 210; London: Oxford University Press, 1940—By permission of the Early English Text Society).

Whole Court Tested in the Person of Sir Gawain

That Gawain is the representative of the court can be shown first by the fact that he takes Arthur's place in answering the Green Knight's challenge, upon the explicit advice and consent of the nobles, to whom Gawain had put the decision when he asked Arthur's permission (ll. 361-65). Second, when he arrives at the castle, Gawain identifies himself by saying that he comes from the court ruled by the noble and courteous Arthur, the powerful royal king of the Round Table (ll. 903-05). Further, repeatedly in this poem, and traditionally in the romances of the Arthurian cycle,[4] Gawain is represented as the most famous member of the Round Table and as the flower of knighthood in a court which itself was the ideal of chivalry. Finally, the reaction of all the men of the Lord's castle, when they realize that the great Gawain is among them, indicates that they consider him to be the representative of Arthur's court *par excellence*; they exalt his excellence, bravery, and refined manners; they hold his fame to be the greatest among all men.

> Þat alle prys & prowes & pured þewes
> Apendes to hys persoun, & praysed is euer;
> By-fore alle men vpon molde his mensk is þe most. (ll. 912-14)

And they rejoice that now they will learn skill in manners and spotless expressions of noble conversation from this father of fine breeding.

> 'Now schal we semlych se sleȝteȝ of þeweȝ
> & þe teccheles termes of talkyng noble;
> Wich spede is in speche, vnspurd may we lerne,
> Syn we haf fonged þat fyne fader of nurture; . . . (ll. 916-19)

The Court Tested for All Its Knightly Qualities

The motive for the coming of the Green Knight and for the subsequent action of the whole poem was Morgan le Fay's desire to test the pride and fame of Arthur's court. Its "pride and fame" could only mean its renown for perfection in chivalry and knighthood, for it

---

[4] William H. Schofield, *English Literature from the Norman Conquest to Chaucer* (New York: The Macmillan Company, 1906), pp. 214-215: "Of all the heroes of British romance, not excepting Arthur himself, Gawain is the most admirable and the most interesting. In the early poems of the cycle he is invariably represented as the mirror of courtesy, a truly noble knight without fear or reproach. His courage was unequalled, his benevolence unbounded, his wisdom acknowledged by all. He was 'the golden tongued,' 'the invincible,' 'gay, gracious, and good.' . . . Arthur loved him most of all his followers, and his companions measured their exploits by his . . . . Nowhere does the irreligious Gawain appear in English literature before the time of Malory. In all sources that present the original saga in its purity, the respect for him is universal, unfeigned, and justified. He was the beloved of all, the envied of none."

was an age of chivalry, and Arthur's court was the foremost representative of the chivalric spirit.

To understand more precisely in what Arthur's court is being tested, we must understand the meaning of chivalry in the Middle Ages. It is a difficult word to define. After examining seven definitions of chivalry, Prestage states that "chivalry is used in a broader sense to include the whole knightly system of the later middle ages, with its peculiar religious, moral, and social codes and customs," and concludes that perhaps Chaucer meant this "when he said of his 'perfight gentil knight' that he 'lovede chyvalrye' with its concomitant 'trouthe and honour, fredom and curteisie'."[5] The inner spirit of this knightly system was the practice of all the chivalric or knightly virtues. The following, selected from Prestage's quotations from four authors[6] and from a Service Book[7] of c. 1000 A.D. describing the investiture ceremony of a knight, seem to be the most prominent knightly virtues: courtesy, generosity, loyalty, truth, honor, courage, fearlessness, deep religious feeling, self-sacrifice, love of adventure, compassion for the weak and oppressed, championing the honor of women, faith, devotion to the Virgin Mary. These may be conveniently grouped under four headings as courtesy, courage, truth or loyalty, and generosity. Chivalry or knighthood, therefore, consists essentially in the practice of courage, courtesy, generosity, and truthfulness or loyalty. It is, apparently, for these knightly virtues or qualities that Arthur's court is tested. The suggestion has been made that the court is being tested in the person of Sir Gawain, and that Gawain is tested in each of his principal virtues. It is clear from the symbolism of the pentangle (the five-pointed figure on his shield) that his virtues are five: generosity, love of his fellow men, purity, chivalry, and piety (ll. 651-54). And from Prestage's synthesis of the common medieval meanings of chivalry, it is likewise clear that three virtues—courage, courtesy, and truth or loyalty—were commonly included in the concept of chivalry. Since chivalry included these three virtues, it is probable that Gawain's virtues would be understood by a medieval man from the symbolism of the pentangle, to be seven in all: generosity, love of fellow men, purity, courtesy, courage, truth, and piety.

[5] Edgar Prestage, *Chivalry: A Series of Studies to Illustrate Its Historical Significance and Civilizing Influence* (London: Kegan Paul, Trench, Trubner and Co., 1928), p. 2. See also William H. Schofield, *Chivalry in English Literature, Chaucer, Malory, Spenser, and Shakespeare* (Cambridge: Harvard University Press, 1912), p. 33. Schofield explains that Chaucer's *trouthe* meant loyalty, and his *fredom* meant *largesse* or generosity.

[6] Prestage, *op. cit.*, pp. 2-3.

[7] *Ibid.*, p. 24.

We may conclude, therefore, that Gawain, and through him the whole court of Arthur, is tested in these seven knightly virtues or qualities in the poem. For Gawain must certainly show generosity and courage when he begs to take Arthur's place in decapitating the Green Knight, when he perseveres through the rigors of winter and the many dangerous adventures in seeking out the Green Knight, and when he finally offers his neck to the axeman. The fact that he accepts the challenge rather than expose Arthur or any of his court to death as well as his kind dealings with the porter and servants in his host's castle testify to his love for his fellow men. His purity, of course, is tested in the triple temptation by his Host's wife and, to a lesser extent, in his joyful dealings with her and her ladies during the day. Gawain's knightly courtesy, too, is sorely tried during the temptations; indeed, on the third morning when the Lady importuned him so continually and pressed him so near to the limit that he was forced either to accept her love or refuse it offensively, the poet explicitly states that Gawain was concerned for his courtesy (ll. 1770-73). To a lesser degree, his courtesy is tested in his dealings with the repulsive old woman, Morgan le Fay, and is constantly "on display" before all the knights and servants. Further, that he obeys his Host in his every wish indicates a form of medieval courtesy—utter obedience of guest to Host.[8] His truth and loyalty are tested especially in the compact with the Host and through the servant who tempts him to turn back from the Green Chapel and to tell men that he could not find the Green Knight. His piety, which surpasses all things according to the Gawain-poet (l. 654: "& pite, þat passeȝ alle poynteȝ") is tested in the most trying circumstances and found true. When lost in the forest on Christmas Eve, he resorts to prayer, asking Christ and Mary to show him a lodging where he might hear Christmas Mass; among the revels of the gay castle, he attends Mass each morning; when he perceives the danger of the first temptation, he blesses himself; in the great danger of the third and strongest temptation, he prays to God and to Mary for help; afterwards he confesses devoutly; and finally, he moves confidently to the Green Chapel after committing himself to God.

---

[8] This form of courtesy is illustrated in several *canzoni* and *exempla*. See Kittredge, *op. cit.*, pp. 93, 96-99.

Gawain's Chastity Especially Tested

It is difficult not to maintain (in agreement with Miss Day and in disagreement with Professor Hulbert) that *Sir Gawain and the Green Knight* is primarily a chastity test.[9] In the first place, it should be remembered that the relationship between Lancelot and Guenever as portrayed in the medieval romances prior to the Gawain-poet was traditionally an adulterous one.[10] It seems likely that the Gawain-poet, knowing this tradition, wished to vindicate Guenever's reputation.[11] In this case it would have been his intention to make the coming of the Green Knight serve also as a test of Guenever's innocence,[12] for one of Morgan le Fay's motives in sending the Knight was to cause Guenever's death by fright (ll. 2459-62). But the fact that Guenever does not die of fright would indicate her innocence, in the Gawain-poet's eyes, of the adulterous charges. A valid conclusion appears to be that Guenever, the Queen of Arthur's court, is being tested for chastity; and since she is a special representative of the court, we may conclude that the whole court is being tested in her person—especially for chastity.

Further evidence for the chastity test as the principal test is the fact that the poet makes Gawain completely victorious in the three Temptations while he allows him to fail in fidelity to his word. The Host also considers the chastity test the most important, for at the Green Chapel he minimizes Gawain's infidelity to his word and emphasizes the fact that it was not for intrigue or wooing that he failed, but for love of his life; hence he is *less* to be blamed. Thus he finds Gawain the most faultless of knights, likening him, when compared to other knights, to a pearl amid white peas.

---

[9] Miss Day, in her introductory essay (Gollancz, *ed. cit.*, p. xxi), argues, against Professor Hulbert, that "Gawain's chief fear is that he may sin against God, and his duty of loyalty to his host takes the second place."

[10] One such romance is Chretien de Troyes' *Le Chevalier de la Charette*, whose central theme is Lancelot's relations with Guenever as lover. Their adulterous relations as pictured in this poem will be treated at length later when we consider the second meaning of the poem.

[11] This wish to vindicate Guenever's reputation will become more clear where it is suggested later in this study that the Gawain-poet's intention is to glorify chastity and to satirize the immoral courtly love portrayed in such romances as Chretien's *Le Chevalier de la Charette*. A further confirmation of the Gawain-poet's desire to vindicate Guenever's reputation is the evidence provided by color symbolism. This evidence will be considered in an analysis of the color symbolism of the poem.

[12] In *The Awntyrs off Arthure*, a middle-fourteenth-century poem, Guenever's mother appears in a thunderstorm and warns her to mend her ways. Wells's comment on this is that "Guenever is now the vain and licentious Queen of later romance, who must be warned of her evil ways." John Edwin Wells, *A Manual of the Writings in Middle English, 1050-1400* (New Haven: Yale University Press, 1916), p. 45.

'I sende hir to asay þe, & sothly me þynkkeȝ,
On þe fautlest freke þat euer on fote ȝede;
As perle bi þe quite pese is of prys more,
So is Gawayn, in god fayth, bi oþer gay knyȝteȝ.
Bot here yow lakked a lyttel, sir, & lewte yow wonted,
Bot þat watȝ for no wylyde werke, ne wowyng nauþer;
Bot for ȝe lufed your lyf, þe lasse I yow blame.' (ll. 2362-68)

Accordingly, the girdle is the emblem of his victory in chastity and not of his defeat in infidelity to his word (though Gawain, true knight, personally considers it an emblem of shame). The Host considers the girdle an emblem of victory, giving it to Gawain with the observation that it will be an excellent token among chivalrous knights of the adventure of the Green Chapel (ll. 2398-99). And the Gawain-poet himself is of the same mind when he remarks at the end of the poem that the girdle was accounted the glory of the Round Table and that whoever after wore it was honored (ll. 2519-20). Even Gawain himself seems to value his chastity most, for in the third temptation, when he is most pressed, he is concerned for his courtesy, but even more for the disaster to him if he should commit sin, and prays God to defend him.

He cared for his cortaysye, lest craþayn he were,
& more for his meschef, ȝif he schulde make synne

.   .   .   .

'God schylde,' quoþ þe schalk, 'þat schal not befalle!' (ll. 1773-76)

Finally, after the second test, when Gawain began to realize the Lady's determination and that he could expect further visits which would endanger his chastity, he asked the Host if he might leave the next morning (ll. 1670-71).

Additional indications that the chastity test is the principal test are the following facts: Gawain saves his life in the beheading test because he was successful in the chastity test; the Challenge is the means of getting Gawain to the castle for the chastity test; and, finally, great emphasis is placed in the poem on Mary, the chaste Virgin—the inner part of Gawain's shield contained an image of the Virgin so that he might frequently look at it and be inspired with never-failing courage; one meaning of the pentangle was the five joys of the gracious queen of heaven, and it is Mary who protects him in the crucial third Temptation (ll. 1768-79: "Gret perile bi-twene hem stod,/Nif Mar[y]e of hir kny3t [con]mynne."). From what has been said it may reasonably be concluded that the first level of meaning of *Sir Gawain and the Green Knight* is the test of Arthur's court, in the person of Gawain, its most exemplary knight, for all its knightly qualities, and especially for chastity.

If this conclusion is valid, it follows that in Gawain's victory in the three temptations and in the other tests of his knightly qualities, the pride and fame of Arthur's court is found true precisely in all its knightly virtues and especially in chastity. But Gawain was found slightly wanting in courage; in fact, his first words when he realizes his infidelity, are a curse upon cowardice and covetousness (l. 2374); therefore, Arthur's court is found slightly wanting in courage. As it was cowardice in fearing for his life which taught Gawain covetousness, which in turn led him to break his faith (ll. 2378-84), so it had been cowardice that made Arthur's court fear to answer the challenge of the Green Knight until the latter had taunted and shamed the knights into action. Accordingly, the girdle, Gawain's symbol of shame, is also the court's symbol of shame. However, we do not feel that its failure is shameful, for both with Gawain and the court the circumstances are so unusual. And the words of the text show that the baldric was worn in token of glorious victory.

> For þat wat3 acorded þe renoun of þe Rounde Table,
> & he honoured þat hit hade, euer-more after, . . . (ll. 2519-20)

Second Level of Meaning

An attempt has been made to point out that the first and more obvious meaning of *Sir Gawain and the Green Knight* is a test of the chivalric virtues of Arthur's court. What follows will attempt, further, to indicate that the second and more subtle meaning amounts to a satire on contemporary romances in their glorification of the adulterous and sentimental code of courtly love and of degenerate chivalry.

The first piece of evidence which points to such contemporary romances as probable objects of the Gawain poet's satire consists in an eight-line passage from the poem itself. Let us consider the pertinent passage. Because it also sheds light on the characteristic qualities of the courtly romances, it is worth quoting in full.

& of alle cheualry to chose, þe chef þyng a-losed
Is þe lel layk of luf, þe lettrure of armes;
F[or] to telle of þis teuelyng of þis trwe kynʒteʒ,
Hit is þe tytelet token & tyxt of her werkkeʒ,
How l[edes] for her lele luf hor lyueʒ han auntered,
Endured for her drury dulful stoundeʒ,
& after wenged with her walour & voyded her care
& broʒt blysse in-to boure with bountees hor awen. (ll. 1512-19) [13]

It is significant that these words, spoken by the Lady to Gawain,
occur in the second Temptation, where she frequently alludes to the
rules of courtesy and love-making. She has been chiding Gawain on
his failure to observe these courtly rules: He has not claimed a kiss
when she gave him a favorable look (ll. 1489-91), nor has he, the
fairest of warriors and the most courteous and knightly of men, spoken
any words which deal with love. Since in her eyes he has thus failed
in knighthood, she will tell him in what chivalry or knighthood really
consists. Its chief part, according to her, is the faithful game of love
(l. 1513: "Is þe lel layk of luf") and the study of fighting, for, she
says, these two are the text of all their works. The "her" (l. 1515) with
"werkkeʒ" refer to the romance writers whom the Lady reads and who
furnish her with her only knowledge of knighthood—her recital of "the
title and text of their works" would be merely a recital of what she
would have read in the courtly romances of her day.

These court romances told of the love of a knight for a lady, of
the fantastic adventures he undertook for her, of the griefs and joys
consequent upon his love. Thus the line, "hor lyueʒ han auntered"
(l. 1516) refers to the many perilous and impossible adventures that
knights undertook at the risk of their lives for their loved one; "Endured
for her drury dulful stoundeʒ" (l. 1517) refers to the "lover's pains"
that knights of such romances suffered because of separation from their
love, or because of her coldness; "& after wenged with her walour &
voyded her care" (l. 1518) indicates how the knights, by their valor,
won their lady, changed her coldness toward them, and thus dispersed

[13] See A. B. Taylor, *The Introduction to the Medieval Romance* (London: Heath Cranton Limited, 1930), p. 236. Taylor gives the following explanation and translation of these lines "to illustrate the supremacy of courtly love; the lady of the castle who offers her love to Gawain reproves him because he has no mistress, and says to him, 'Of all chivalry, the chief part is love, the literature of arms; it is the title and test of their works, how men for their loved ones have endangered their lives, endured great hardships, avenged them with valour, removed their sorrow, and brought bliss into the bower'."

their grief and suffering; and, finally, "& broȝt blysse in-to boure" (l. 1519) refers to the crowning reward for their devotion, the pleasure of the body of their lady.[14]

We may conclude that in this passage the Lady refers to the contemporary courtly romances. It may be concluded, further—on the supposition of a satiric intention—that, in representing his hero as being inexpert in the "game of love" as outlined in the romances, the Gawain-poet wishes to make these romances the object of his criticism.

The second piece of evidence pointing to the courtly romances as objects of satire is the striking contrast between *Sir Gawain and the Green Knight* and any one of the courtly romances. Since the most typical of these romances, and the one which exercised the greatest influence on all subsequent romances, was Chretien's *Le Chevalier de la Charette*,[15] a comparison between this work and *Sir Gawain and the Green Knight* will make more evident the probability of the Gawain-poet's satire of courtly romances.

The most striking difference between the two poems is the Christian atmosphere of genuine piety and of chastity which pervades *Sir Gawain and the Green Knight* and the surface piety and the condonation of adultery under a ridiculous code of external ideals of behavior[16] which characterize *Le Chevalier de la Charette*. Thus, in the Gawain-poet's masterpiece, the motive force of all Gawain's actions is his knightly ideal of honor, of chastity, of loyalty to his word, and of love for Mary; in Chretien's poem, the motive deciding every deed of Lancelot is his love for Guenever. Gawain refuses to sin with the Lady because of his love for Mary and his love of chastity; but Lancelot refuses to sin with the damsel who offered him a night's lodging only because he is pledged to Guenever. Moreover, Gawain's religion is genuine

---

14 In this context the joy of bower can only mean the delights of illicit love; for this is what the Lady has frankly asked Gawain to teach her while her husband is away.

15 According to its title, it is the story of a knight (Lancelot) who degraded his knighthood by riding on a cart meant for criminals, because his love for Guenever demanded such a deed; but its real theme is the illicit love between Lancelot and Guenever. Because the poem professedly sets out to illustrate the practice and conventions of courtly love and because it is the literary source of so many other courtly romances, it may be taken as the best representative of its kind. The Gawain-poet was probably familiar with this poem; in any event, it can scarcely be doubted that he knew the many romances this poem influenced. The passage quoted above (ll. 1512-19) and the whole tenor of the Lady's remarks about love in the Temptations reflect his knowledge of the courtly conventions. See P. G. Thomas, *English Literature Before Chaucer* (London: Edward Arnold and Co., 1924), p. 135. Thomas says that "no poet of the period excelled him in knowledge of courtly diction and convention...."

16 In many of the romances Arthur, together with his whole court, condones the adulterous relation between Guenever and Lancelot. See Wells, *op. cit.*, p. 29.

and is the dominating force in his life; Lancelot's religion, on the other hand, is merely a form and does not influence his practical life. Thus when Gawain attends Mass at Camelot before leaving for his quest, and at the Castle during his Christmas stay, he draws strength for his combat; but Lancelot attends Mass only because it is one of the functions going on in a given castle at which he happens to be staying. This obvious contrast between *Sir Gawain and the Green Knight* and *Le Chevalier de la Charette* suggests that the Gawain-poet is satirizing the courtly romances of which Chretien's poem is representative.

Another difference between the two poems is the contrasting standard of values which, respectively, the Gawain-poet and Chretien use. The Gawain-poet considers chastity to be the basic virtue of a knight; Gawain, consequently, is allowed to fail somewhat in courage in accepting the girdle and in flinching at the Green Knight's axe-stroke, but he is heroic in the preservation of his chastity. On the other hand, Chretien disregarded chastity but glorified knightly courage in defense of a lady. Lancelot is utterly fearless in his many battles and in the superhuman pain involved in crossing the sword-bridge, but he fails completely in chastity.

The fact that the Gawain-poet allows his ideal knight to fail in a virtue which the courtly romancers prized so highly, and that he makes his hero a model of chastity in defiance of their exaltation of adulterous love, likewise suggests satire. These romances glorified the almost superhuman courage of knights at the expense of more basic virtues. The Gawain-poet exhibits more balance. He will allow failure in less important qualities but insists on the more basic virtue of chastity. This insistence seems by contrast to constitute a criticism of the courtly romances.

The satiric intention of the Gawain-poet becomes clearer upon further consideration of the glorified code of courtly love which is quite obviously referred to by the Lady in the passage already quoted. This code is exhibited and, so this study maintains, satirized under three main aspects: adulterous love, deification of women, and absurd sentimentality. A very brief study of the code of courtly love will clarify the satiric aim.

The Code of Courtly Love originated in a brilliant, woman-dominated society of eleventh-century southern France where mock courts of love decided matters of love according to definite rules governing the sexes. The amorous duchess, Eleanor of Aquitaine, introduced the doctrines and practices of the court into northern France, where women of high rank espoused these ideas and were responsible for their advent into contemporary literature through the troubadours. These latter, wandering knight-minstrels, sang their songs to the noble married ladies of each court, "extolling their beauties, professing most passionate love and devotion, portraying the anguish caused by neglect and delay, and begging in the plainest terms for the alleviation of these sufferings."[17] Such a singer, Chretien de Troyes, received the courtly ideas from Marie of Champagne and introduced them into the Round Table romances which, under his hands, "became the representatives *par excellence* of the chivalrous and courtly ideal of the twelfth century society."[18]

The abstract principles and laws underlying the courtly system may be reduced to four:[19] (1) courtly love is sensual;[20] (2) courtly love is illicit, and for the most part, adulterous;[21] (3) courtly love must be secret, for a love which is divulged rarely lasts; and (4) courtly love must not be too easily obtained.[22]

The lady in such an artificial system is deified. She is "represented as perfect in all her attributes, especially in her physical beauty, character, and influence on others."[23] Her hair is golden, "her eyes beautiful, complexion fresh and clear, mouth rosy and smiling, flesh white, soft, and smooth, body slender, well formed, without blemish. In character she is distinguished for her courtesy, kindness, refinement and good sense."[24] Through her influence, which is always ennobling, her lover becomes courteous, gentle, humble, generous, and courageous.

Such a system, in which "love was an art to be practiced rather than a passion to be felt,"[25] was largely a matter of behavior, of

---

[17] Lewis Freeman Mott, *The System of Courtly Love Studied as an Introduction to the Vita Nuova of Dante* (New York: G. E. Stechert and Co., 1924), p. 3.

[18] William G. Dodd, *Courtly Love in Chaucer and Gower* ("Harvard Studies in English, I"; Cambridge: Harvard University Press, 1913), p. 2. The brief sketch given in the present study of the origins of courtly love is drawn mainly from the first several pages of Dodd's excellent study.

[19] These rules are taken from Dodd, *ibid.*, p. 7.

[20] *Loc. cit.*

[21] *Loc. cit.* Andreas Capellanus (*De Arte Honeste Amandi*) is quoted: "Dicimus enim et stabilito tenore firmamus, amorem non posse suas inter duos iugales extendere vires."

[22] John F. Rowbotham, *The Troubadours and Courts of Love* (London: Swan Sonnenshein and Co., 1896), p. 246: "Too easy possession renders love contemptible. But possession which is attended with difficulties makes love valuable and of great price." Rule 14 of Andreas' 31 Laws of Love.

[23] Dodd, *op. cit.*, p. 10.

[24] *Loc. cit.*

[25] Dodd, *op. cit.*, p. 3.

regulating one's conduct by the strict rules[26] and restrictions of the code. Naturally the literature which drew its inspiration from such love was devoid of real feeling and became "characterized by artificiality and monotony of sentiment."[27]

From this very brief sketch it is easy to recognize the three-fold aspect of the courtly love code which the Gawain-poet appears chiefly to satirize: adulterous love, the deification of women, and absurd sentimentality. In *Sir Gawain and the Green Knight* the lady, who represents the norm and standards of this code, is made to appear ridiculous when, unrepresentative of her type, she takes the offensive in adulterous love-making, and when, being rebuffed by Gawain, she becomes sentimental. Gawain, also unrepresentative of his type, represents the norm of chastity and appears always the knight of restraint and common sense. Realization of these unrepresentative roles of the lady and Gawain is indispensable for an understanding of the poem as a satire against the courtly love usually portrayed in the romances.

Almost certain evidence of satire against the adultery of the code is Gawain's stinging retort to the Lady's suggestion that were she to bargain and choose to get herself a husband (ll. 1271-75), she would choose the beautiful and courteous Gawain (l. 1276: " 'I-wysse, worþy,' quoþ þe wyȝe, 'ȝe haf waled wel better' "), that is, you have chosen much better because you already have a husband, and it is much better that you persevere in your choice. The adulterous code is again the point in Gawain's criticism of the Lady's frank approval of adultery. This approval is reflected, first, in her statements that her husband is away (ll. 1230-31; 1534); secondly, in her desire for secrecy, when she asks Gawain not to tell her husband about the girdle she has given him (ll. 1862-63); and again, when she tempts Gawain with the remark that 'we are but alone" (l. 1230). Finally, the code is further criticized in the person of the Lady's husband, the Host, who represents marital fidelity; for the Host accounts Gawain's acceptance and concealment of the girdle as a trifling fault and reserves all his praises for him because he was faithful against his wife's intrigue (ll. 2364-67). In

---

[26] *Ibid.*, p. 11. The lover must show his passion by the following symptoms which soon came to be necessary constituents of love: suffering or severe sickness, sleeplessness, confusion and loss of speech in the lady's presence, trembling and pallor when near the one beloved, etc.

[27] *Ibid.*, p. 3.

the traditional courtly romance the husband was either unaware of or indifferent to his wife's infidelities.

There is a twofold evidence for satire against the code's deification of woman: Gawain's remark about the deceit of women, and the degraded position of the lady throughout the temptation scenes. While Gawain is burning with shame at being found false in concealing the girdle, he speaks of Adam, Solomon, Samson, and David—all deceived by the wiles of women (ll. 2414-19)—and concludes that it were best to love but not to believe them (ll. 2420-21).

Satire against the deification of women is inferred from the completely reversed positions of the Lady and the Man in the Temptation scenes. When she should, according to the courtly love code, be the cruel, cold mistress spurning the pathetic advances of her lover,[28] the Lady instead takes the offensive, asks for a kiss, proposes to be his servant, and offers her body to him; and for her advances she is, in the second temptation, sharply told to stop such talk (l. 1492: " 'Do way,' quoþ þat derf mon, 'my dere, þat speche,' "). When her love is spurned, she sets to complaining and lamenting—traditional traits of the agonized *male* lover. When she should be the queen dispensing kisses as favors, she asks Gawain's permission to kiss him and thereby suffers the humiliation of hearing him say that she may kiss him when she likes and cease when she likes.[29] When she should be the great teacher of the art of love and of its ennobling effects on her lover, she herself asks to be taught the art of love and debases herself by asking Gawain if he considers her too stupid to learn (l. 1529: " 'Oþer elles ʒe demen me to dille your dalyaunce to herken?' "), after he has refused to tell her of arms and war and true love. The awful implication is that she is not capable of understanding *true* love. And when she should be the apotheosis of courtesy, she appears to be satirized for her bold intrusion into Gawain's chamber by Gawain's reminder that compulsion is considered unlucky in his land (l. 1499: " 'Bot þrete is vn-þryuande in þede þer I lende' "); that is, Gawain is saying that where

---

28 In Chretien's poem, Guenever is such a mistress; she refused to see Lancelot—even after he had undergone unbelievable hardships to free her—because his momentary hesitation before jumping on the cart implied imperfection in his love for her.

29 We can hardly imagine Chretien's Lancelot, the courtly slave to his mistress (he did his worst in the tournament at her command) and the courtly votary to his goddess (he treated her room as a shrine), speaking so authoritatively and harshly to Guenever. It should be noted that Gawain's treatment of the Lady in the Temptations is as much a satire on any courtly knight of the type of Lancelot as is the Lady's ridiculous reversal of position a satire on the courtly lady of the romances.

he lives, he would not think of compelling another against his or her
will; and satire is indicated by his suggestion that every gift not
made with good will (l. 1500: " '& vche gift þat is geuen not wiþ
goud wylle' ") is likewise considered unlucky—Gawain implying here
that her gift of herself to him is prompted by bad will. She is further
ridiculed when she attributes it to God's grace that she has him whom
all desire, by Gawain's ironical remark that he has found her generosity
noble (that is, he has found her selfishness ignoble) and by his invoca-
tion of Mary, the guardian of chastity, to reward her for such a noble
deed of hers (asking for adulterous love).

'Bot I louue þat ilk lorde þat þe lyfte haldeȝ,
I haf hit holly in my honde þat al desyres,
                    þurȝe grace.'

.   .   .   .

'Madame,' quoþ þe myry mon, 'Mary yow ȝelde,
For I haf founden, in god fayth, yowre frau$n$chis nobele. . . .' (ll. 1256-64)

This Lady is a far remove from the exalted goddess who rules unchal-
lenged in the code of courtly love.

The sentimental and artificial love of the court is exposed in the
Lady's reaction to Gawain's refusal of her love: She says that she is
wounded in heart more than all the creatures in the world (l. 1781:
" 'Bifore alle þe wyȝeȝ in þe worlde wounded in hert' ") and that she
can only mourn in life as a maid who loves greatly (l. 1795: " 'I may
bot mourne vpon molde, as may þat much louyes' "); and at parting
from Gawain, she asks for the consolation of a gift, a glove perhaps,
just as a love-sick knight would ask his "noble" lady-love for a lock
of her hair that he might treasure it with adoring sighs. Indeed, the
Lady's whole conception of love seems to be sentimental; she says that
the other ladies would like to possess him to play pleasantly with his
charming words that they might obtain comfort and assuage their
troubles (ll. 1253-54: " 'To daly wiþ derely your daynte wordeȝ,
/Keuer hem comfort & colen her careȝ' "). The fact that Gawain, the
embodiment of common sense in contrast to the sentimentality of the
Lady, is quite unsympathetic with her emotions, amounts to a satire on
her sentimentality, as well as on that of the traditionally sentimental
male lovers of the romances.

The same eight-line text, which points to contemporary romances
as objects of the Gawain-poet's satire, also indicates the degenerate conception of chivalry which the courtly romances portrayed and which,
it may be validly inferred, was likewise the over-all object of this satire.

COLOR SYMBOLISM IN *SIR GAWAIN*

The passage is worth quoting again.

'& of alle cheualry to chose, þe chef þyng a-losed
Is þe lel layk of luf, þe lettrure of armes;
F[or] to telle of þis teuelyng of þis trwe knyȝteȝ,
His is þe tytelet token & tyxt of her werkkeȝ,
How l[edes] for her lele luf hor lyueȝ han auntered,
Endured for her drury dulful stoundeȝ,
& after wenged with her walour & voyded her care
& broȝt blysse in-to boure with bountees hor awen.' (ll. 1512-19)

These lines, as already noted, are part of the Lady's lengthy plea to Gawain that he teach her the sport of love (ll. 1508-34). We recall that she had complained to him that he, the outstanding example of courtesy and knighthood, had not taught her of love. The logic behind her complaint is revealing. She considers the game of love to be the chief element in chivalry; for the mighty deeds and dangerous adventures of which the romancers sing in their works are motivated solely by the knights' love for their ladies[30] and their hope for the joys of bower as reward. In this plea of the Lady, the Gawain-poet is setting forth a picture of the degenerate chivalry portrayed by so many romancers. Knights went on fantastic adventures, fought valiantly to free enchanted princesses, and were admitted to their beds by night. Or else, as in the case of Lancelot, a knight championed a married woman with whom he enjoyed as reward the "joy of bower"—practices far removed from the ideal of true knighthood blessed by the Church in a solemn rite.[31] The satire in this passage is discoverable in the Lady's perverted idea of true knighthood. She persists in speaking of Gawain as the most *knightly*, she begs him to teach her of *true* love, she considers that the knights of the romances risk their loves for *true* love, and in the same breath she asks Gawain to commit adultery while her husband is away. Gawain himself shows us how we are to interpret this plea of the Lady and reveals his attitude toward the chivalry she describes. When he speaks about taking on himself the *hard* task of expounding *true* love (l. 1540), we feel at once the lie given to the "faithful game of love," which the Lady says is conspicuous in all chivalry, and to the emptiness of the deeds of the men who risk their

---

[30] Rule 26 of Andreas Capellanus' 31 Laws of Love is: "Love can deny nothing to love." Rowbotham, *op. cit.*, p. 247.

[31] See Charles Sears Baldwin, *An Introduction to English Medieval Literature* (London: Longmans, Green and Co., 1922), pp. 68-69: "All night before the altar he kept vigil over his armor. In the morning, after Mass, he vowed to serve God and his lady, to protect all women, to succor the distressed."

lives for lady-loves and illicit joys. And Gawain considers that it would be a folly for him to explain to her the themes of the texts and tales of arms (l. 1541), that is, the themes of those works which he esteems so slightly.

Finally, by the subtle means of making Gawain the mirror of perfect Christian knighthood and the glory of chivalry, the Gawain-poet seems to satirize a chivalry[32] that differs vastly from that which Gawain personally represents. There can be no doubt that Gawain represents the flower of true chivalry. The Host considers him this when he likens him to a pearl of great price (ll. 2364-65: "As perle bi þe quite pese is of prys more,/So is Gawayn in god fayth, bi oþer gay kny3te."). All acknowledge him the perfect, courteous knight; his shield symbolizes this; and Gawain himself meets every test except one in the poem.

Satirical Import of the Poem

A careful analysis shows that the poem represents a test of Arthur's court, in the person of Gawain, for all the knightly virtues, but especially for chastity. Comparison of the poem with *Le Chevalier de la Charette* as a representative example of the courtly romances indicates that the Gawain-poet has satirized the decay of the chivalric virtues and especially chastity in the code of courtly love.

We are now in a position to state the complete meaning of the poem. The Gawain-poet wished to write a genuinely Christian poem to glorify true Christian chivalry in which the virtue of chastity held the foremost place. His use of courtly love in *Sir Gawain and the Green Knight* and the great contrast in tone between his poem and Chretien's suggest that he heartily disliked the type of romance which used the court of Arthur and its heroes as a framework[33] in which to revel in the

---

[32] Such a degenerate chivalry is that of the courtly romances, in which knights were more concerned with paramours than with genuine knightly deeds. There seems to be a deliberate attempt in *Sir Gawain* to build the character of Gawain in conscious contrast with knights like Chretien's Lancelot. Thus, from what is known of him in the poem, we are confident that Gawain would not have lost his color and powers of speech or have come close to swooning, as Lancelot does when he sees a comb containing strands of Guenever's golden hair; or be so heedless of true knighthood, as was Lancelot when he became so preoccupied with thoughts of Guenever that he failed to hear a knight's triple challenge and was consequently knocked from his horse.

[33] Guenever's traditional adulterous relations with Lancelot, and the jealousy these relations aroused in Morgan le Fay, gave the Gawain-poet the motive force for the coming of the Green Knight; it provided him also with the opportunity to emphasize chastity and its testing in the poem.

immoral courtly love conventions. As interpreted, then, the Gawain-poet wished to reestablish the court of Arthur as the model of true knighthood and to show that chastity must be an important virtue in any genuine chivalry.[34] To achieve this end, he chose Gawain, the most famous and most unstained of all Arthurian heroes, to be his ideal knight and the representative of Arthur's court. And since the most convincing proof of the solid worth of anything is to subject it to trial, the Gawain-poet devised the various tests for Gawain. In Gawain's successful meeting of all the tests of chivalry, Arthur's court was seen to be the model of chivalry. Because, however, the greatest blot on the Arthurian court, according to the old romancers, was Guenever's marital infidelity, this stain had first to be removed.[35] Hence, we suggest that this is another reason why Gawain's test is primarily a chastity test. In this test he is totally successful. And in his success Guenever and the whole Arthurian court are proved innocent. The poem is thus a test of chastity and of all the old chivalric virtues; and through victory in these tests the poet greatly glorifies chastity and genuine Christian chivalry.[36]

The further purpose of this study is to consider, first, whether the use of color in *Sir Gawain and the Green Knight* is symbolical; and secondly, if color is so used, what it symbolizes. Answers to these questions will reveal whether the use of color harmonizes with the interpretation of the poem already suggested and whether it clarifies and gives a richer meaning to this interpretation.

Non-Color Symbolism

It should first be noted that there are three instances of the use of non-color symbolism in *Sir Gawain and the Green Knight,* that of the pentangle, of the hunting scenes, and of precious stones. The Gawain-poet himself, even at the risk of delaying the narrative (l. 624: " 'I am *in*-tent yow to telle, þof tary hyt me schulde' "), devotes fifty-two lines in careful explanation of the pentangle. Its symbolism, as well as the special symbolism of the diamonds Gawain wears about his head and the pearls the Lady wears, will be noted later.

---

[34] One of the virtues symbolized on the pentangle of his shield is chastity.

[35] Guenever is also shown to be innocent because she does not die of fright at the sight of the Green Knight; according to Morgan le Fay's test, she would have died of fear had she been guilty.

[36] The point is not that chastity was in the Middle Ages actually the foremost virtue of chivalry—even of Christian chivalry; it is merely that the Gawain-poet, disapproving of the sentimental and adulterous knights of the courtly romances, wrote a poem of Christian chivalry in which he purposely gave chastity a dominant part.

The symbolism of the three hunting scenes, however, demands a fuller explanation at this time. In an excellent article Henry Savage shows that the Temptation and the Hunting scenes are bound together not only by the "exchange of winnings compact," but "also by a certain parallelism in their situations which would probably be quite apparent to the lady or gentleman of the fourteenth century."[37] Savage believes that "the key to an understanding of the *raison d'être* of the hunting scenes lies . . . in the attitude of the medieval hunter and herald towards the several beasts whose chase the poem records."[38] From heraldry we learn that the peculiar traits and attributes of the hart and boar make them noble game and beasts of venery; thus they are frequently used in shield forms, while the fox, because of his reputation for cunning and duplicity, is considered a beast of chase (a beast to be hunted out and destroyed, as vermin) and is, accordingly, rarely met with in British heraldry.[39]

The Lady, we recall, is unsuccessful in tempting Gawain the first and second days. Like the game her husband pursues in the forest, Gawain is "noble" because he remains faithful.[40] But on the third day he breaks his "forwarde" and is guilty of being false to his knightly word and deceitful to a generous and trusting host; "a false beast is roused in the forest, and a false man revealed in the castle; a sly fox is caught in the wood, a 'sly fox' in the castle."[41] Savage also indicates how the traditional characteristics of the hart, the boar, and the fox parallel Gawain's conduct in the temptations. Thus, as the hart exhibits "great quickness of hearing to foreknow his hazards"[42] and "great caution . . . in knowing what to avoid and when to avoid it,"[43] so Gawain in the first temptation is cautious and evasive (he feigns sleep). Again, as the boar is known for fierceness, violence, bold spirit, high resolution to "die valorously in the Field" rather than "to secure himself by ignominious Flight,"[44] so Gawain in the second temptation is more bold, meets danger head-on, and even rebukes the Lady. Finally, as the fox is a

---

[37] Henry L. Savage, "The Significance of the Hunting Scenes in Sir Gawain and the Green Knight," *JEGP*, XXVII (1928), 1.

[38] *Loc. cit.*

[39] John Woodward and George Burnett, *A Treatise on Heraldry* (Edinburgh and London: W. & A. K. Johnston, 1892), I, 230.

[40] Savage, *op. cit.*, p. 5.

[41] *Loc. cit.*

[42] John Gullim, *A Display of Heraldry* (London: 1724), p. 156.

[43] Savage, *op. cit.*, p. 9.

[44] Gullim, *op. cit.*, p. 165.

"false beast ... so cunning and subtle that neither men nor hounds can find a remedy to keep themselves from false turns,"[45] so Gawain in the third temptation, like the fox who makes a false turn to avoid the sharp blade, resorts to the false turn of accepting the girdle in order to avoid the impending blow from the Green Knight.[46]

Color Symbolism in General

So much evidence of symbolic parallels suggests that the Gawain-poet may have been more interested in symbolism than has been generally recognized—particularly in color symbolism, since color appears so frequently in this poem.[47] The probability of this interest is all the greater in the light of the widespread symbolic use of color during the medieval period, discussed in the first part of this study.

Analysis of the poem itself reveals, first, the tremendous emphasis put on the color green. Several heroes in the old myths and romances were entirely black or red or green, but not one is totally green—skin, beard, and hair, or possesses a totally green horse, as is the case with the Green Knight.[48] Analysis shows, secondly, that despite the lavish use of color in the poem, a definite restraint is evident in the use of color for natural description. In the beautiful passage on the passing of the seasons, the only color mentioned is the greenness of the grounds and of the grass turning to gray; and during Gawain's travels from Arthur's court to the castle, and from the castle to the Green Chapel, the only color words are the conventional white boiling brooks and white snow. This restraint is also evident generally in the descriptions of clothing and armor. Frequently clothes, rich tapestry, and precious stones are spoken of in such general terms as "most brilliant, bright, most precious gems," but no definite color is used. Obviously, in such instances, the poet desires to give the impression of richness without the use of an explicit color. An attempt will be made to point out how, in other instances, the use of definite colors may be symbolic.

The aim here is not to claim apodictically that the Gawain-poet consciously intended this or that color usage as a definite symbol; it is simply to indicate that certain traditionally symbolic color meanings are

---

[45] See Savage, *op. cit.,* p. 4.

[46] *Ibid.,* p. 6.

[47] According to Alice E. Pratt, *The Use of Color in the Verse of the English Romantic Poets,* p. 115, there are 111 actual color words and 132 color images in the poem, or 43.9 color words and 52.2 color images per 100 lines in *Sir Gawain and the Green Knight.* The Gawain-poet's contemporary, Chaucer, has only fourteen color words per 100 lines in his works, according to Miss Pratt, *op. cit.,* p. 115.

[48] Kittredge, *op. cit.,* p. 142.

strikingly appropriate to the interpretation of the basic meaning of the poem and that there is a striking consistency in the use of these symbolic colors throughout the poem. Even independently of such internal evidence, it is highly probable that color is used symbolically in this poem because of the Gawain-poet's love for symbolism in general and because of his knowledge of the code of color symbolism as it existed in the Middle Ages, especially in Dante, in the *Roman de la Rose* (that medieval treasury of symbolism and conventional love), and in Chaucer, his contemporary.[49]

Part One—Arrival of the Green Knight

This first part of the poem has its setting in Arthur's great hall and deals primarily with the visit of the Green Knight. But before the entrance of this remarkable personage, there occurs the significant use of the color gray, the very first color to be used in the entire poem. In a piece of literature, the first, as well as the last positions, are usually considered significant. The first and last colors used in *Sir Gawain and the Green Knight*—the *gray* eyes of Guenever and the *green* girdle which all the court of Arthur wears as a baldric in honor of Gawain—may, therefore, be considered significant as clues to the interpretation of the basic meaning of the poem as primarily a chastity test. We shall see, in Part Four of the poem, that the green baldric is worn in perpetual commemoration of Gawain's victory in the chastity test; here, in Part One, the color of Guenever's eyes is most significant because it suggests that she is innocent of Morgan le Fay's accusation of adulterous dealings.

Guenever's Gray Eyes

Curry tells us that gray eyes were, above all, beautiful eyes. "In fact, grey seems at times to have lost any definite significance it may orginally have had, and to be merely a synonym for beautiful or bright or radiant."[50] He cites the examples of many knights and ladies of romance, history, and legend who have gray eyes. It is to be noted that when gray means merely beautiful in the romances, it is as a rule used in a passage where the whole face—red lips, gay mouth, golden hair, and so on—is

[49] Coolidge Otis Chapman, "Virgil and the Gawain-Poet," *PMLA*, LX (1945), 16: "Of the books he [Gawain-poet] certainly knew, the Vulgate is of first importance for its influence upon the poet's thought and style. Certain, but less important, are the *Romance of the Rose*, and the French text of Mandeville. Of the books very probably read by him, the *Divine Comedy* stands first...."

[50] Walter Clyde Curry, *The Middle English Ideal of Personal Beauty* (Baltimore: J. H. Furst Company, 1916), p. 51.

described; in *Sir Gawain and the Green Knight*, the poet acknowledges
the Lady's superlative beauty and notes only one detail (ll. 82-83:
"Þe comlokest to discrye/Þer glent wiþ yȝen gray"). The use of gray
as synonymous with beauty does not exclude a symbolic use of gray in a
given romance in which evidence of poetic intention indicates a symbolic
use. Does such evidence appear in *Sir Gawain and the Green Knight?*
According to the incident narrated by Froissart, one of the symbolic
uses of gray is innocence accused.[51] Karl le Rouge had accused Jacques
de Gris of having seduced his daughter. The medieval reader immediately recognized Jacques' total innocence, for, in the familiar language
of symbolism, le Rouge (red) signifies blood and vengeance, and Gris
(gray), innocence accused. Traditionally, Guenever had likewise been
accused of adulterous relations with Lancelot. Accordingly, when
Morgan le Fay devised the Green Knight test to frighten Guenever to
death, she virtually accused her of infidelity. Because, however, Guenever
does not die of fright, and because Gawain, who represents the court of
which she is a member, is victorious in his chastity test, it would seem
that the Gawain-poet is suggesting that Guenever, too, is innocent. If
we recall the accepted medieval symbolic meaning for gray, it is reasonable to suppose that the medieval reader, as in the case of Jacques de
Gris, would immediately have recognized Guenever's innocence under
accusation.

The Green Knight

Certainly the most striking feature of the knight is his brilliant green
color (ll. 235-236: "As growe grene as þe gres & grener hit
semed,/Þen grene aumayl on golde [g]lowande bryȝter"). Nearly as
striking, however, is the constant combination of green and gold in the
descriptions of the Knight. His neat hose are green, his spurs of bright
gold; his sword is of green steel and hammered gold; gold is ever in the
middle of all the intricate designs and patterns on his green dress and
saddle; and even the green hairs of the horse's mane, tail, and forelock
are mingled and braided with gold thread. Green and gold are definitely
the Knight's distinctive colors.

Among the many symbolic meanings of green in the Middle Ages,
four predominate: hope, life and immortality, chastity, and the preternatural. We recall that the first two meanings arose from the yearly
phenomenon of the rebirth of life in nature and from men's sure hope

---

[51] See p. 29 of this study.

of this earthly rebirth as well as the hope of rebirth in eternal life. We likewise recall that green meant chastity to Chaucer and the preternatural in the ballads. There is little doubt that, owing to his great size, unusual color, and the antics he performs with his head, the Green Knight is recognized as a preternatural being. (The brave Arthurian court is dazed into silent wonder and fear at his aspect and at his challenge.) However, as we perceive later in the poem, the other three meanings have a very proper place. For the Green Knight leads Gawain to a chastity test, in which he will prove victorious and because of which he will save his *life* and gain *immortal* renown. Here we meet the first occurence of a common usage of color symbolism in the poem —foreshadowing. Green is the color of hope, and the Green Knight thus hints to Gawain that he can *hope* for success in the quest. When the Green Knight learns that it is Gawain who has accepted his challenge, he shows by his favorable words that his intentions are not malicious, for he tells Gawain that he is exceedingly anxious and pleased that it is Gawain who strikes the blow.

> 'Sir Gawan, so mot I þryue,
> As I am ferly fayn
> Þis dint þat þou schal dryue.'
> 'Bi gog,' quoþ þe grene knyȝt, '*sir* Gawan, me lykes
> Þat I schal fange at þy fust þat I haf frayst here;...' (ll. 387-91)

Gold, because of its worth and purity, signifies personal integrity, honor, and goodness, as is clear from its use in heraldry, in Dante's *Paradiso,* and in some of Chaucer's tales. As a talisman it brought happiness and prosperity. The gold on the Green Knight symbolizes his integrity or non-malicious intent; it also indicates that the knight, who is brave and bold enough to accept his challenge, is undertaking an adventure of great worth and productive of great glory, but one which demands, likewise, personal worth and integrity. Gold and green together symbolize the reasonable hope of accomplishing a *noble* deed and establish the Green Knight as a "trust-worthy" person.

The Green Knight is given two other colors, red and white. The green robe which he wears over his green coat is lined with shining white fur. We recall from the medieval color sequences, which regulated the colors of vestments to be used in the Church worship, and from Dante's and Chaucer's usage, that white symbolizes chastity, truth and honesty, and victory. We have here another case of foreshadowing. Though the Knight may present a fearful external aspect, yet his true meaning is to be discovered within. The white fur tells the reader that the Green

Knight is to be the instrument of the chastity test, that his challenge is an honest one, that he himself will not deceive, and that Gawain may expect to be victorious.

Finally, in the dramatic moment after he has made the challenge, and while deep silence reigns in Arthur's court, the Green Knight bends in his saddle, sweeps his shining green beard from side to side, and rolls his red eyes about horribly. We recall that red in medieval usage frequently had a sinister connotation—for example, Judas was represented with a red beard. Red is used here, of course, to make the Knight appear more terrible. But since red, in the language of heraldry, means personal courage, it may also signify the courage of the warlike Knight who so utterly defies Arthur's court, and who challenges the courage of that court, as well as Gawain's own courage in accepting the challenge.

Among the other color symbolisms of red in Part One are Arthur's blushes of shame and anger before the taunts of the Green Knight at the cowardice of the court. This is significant because the court has just been tested and found momentarily guilty of fear; and Arthur's blush of shame indicates that he realizes this.

Part Two—Gawain Arrives at the Castle

Gawain's Colors

This second part takes Gawain from Arthur's court to the castle and puts all in readiness for the chastity test. The first symbolic use of color in this part is found in the arming scene, in which Gawain fastens about his neck a tunic lined with white fur. The white symbolizes that Gawain is, through and through, pure and chaste and of unstained virtue. And just as the white lining of the Green Knight's cloak symbolizes that he is the instrument of Gawain's chastity test and foreshadows that Gawain will be triumphant, so Gawain's white lining identifies him as the one tested and suggests his triumph in the challenge test. It is significant that the clothes of no other persons in the poem are lined with white. This similarity of color in the white lining of their clothes separates, by means of the language of color symbolism, the Knight and Gawain, tester and tested, from the other persons, and suggests the fact that they are the principal characters.

Like the Green Knight, Gawain is resplendent in gold. He has gold spurs, his knee armor is attached with gold, even the smallest latchet or loop of his armor shines with gold. The Saddle of Gringolet (Gawain's Steed) gleams with gold fringes; the bridle is trimmed with bright gold;

"and there was everywhere, set on red, gold nails" (1. 603).[52] This last sentence indicates that Gawain's steed wore a red cloth of some kind. And Gawain's shield is bright red (1. 620: "Wyth þe pentangel de-paynt of pure golde hweȝ"). The knot of the pentangle, called the endless knot by the English (1. 629), is fashioned to the shield (1. 663: "Ryally wyth red golde vpon rede gowleȝ").

Thus Gawain, like the Green Knight, has his two distinguishing colors, gold and red. The gold again signifies his personal worth and integrity of character; the Gawain-poet himself suggests this meaning when he likens Gawain to refined gold because he is free from every discourtesy and graced with virtues among men (ll. 633-34: "Gawan watȝ for gode knawen & as golde pured,/Voyded of vche vylany, wyth vertueȝ ennourned in mote"). This meaning is verified by the symbolism of the pentangle or endless knot. As each angle of the knot is joined to each other in such a way that it has no end and is nowhere incomplete or separated, so Gawain's five virtues are joined to each other in such a way as to form in him an integrated and totally virtuous character. And the red, since its use on the shield is heraldic, will tell something of the renown of its wearer. As the background color of the shield, it indicates that the basic stuff of Gawain's character is his great courage and valor and his utter self-sacrifice for others. Secondarily, the background red of the shield may symbolize the suffering and the temptation to sin that his adventure will bring him; for we have seen that the Church prescribed red for the feasts of martyrs to signify their suffering and martyrdom and that the stained-glass in Chartres Cathedral gives the devil who tempts Jesus red skin. Its over-all symbolism, however, is probably that of the nobility and courage of its wearer.

Finally, the circlet around Gawain's head is full of precious diamonds and furnishes an example of gem symbolism. The diamond, a brilliantly white and transparent stone, is primarily the symbol of innocence and purity.[53] Worn around the head, it symbolizes in particular Gawain's pure thoughts and, in general, the purity and excellence of his life—for it is the head which guides and directs man's actions.

The Castle

As Gawain approaches the castle after his hectic two months of adventures, color, unmentioned during his journeys, is suddenly reintro-

---

[52] This is the translation given in the notes to the text of Gollancz, p. 105.
[53] Henry Turner Bailey, *Symbolism for Artists, Creative and Appreciative* (Worcester, Mass.: The Davis Press, 1925), p. 90.

duced. White is the distinguishing color of the castle and its environs. At the foot of high hills, one hundred very great hoar (white or light gray) oaks stand guard at the entrance into the swamp and mist that lie before the castle. After his prayer to Christ and Our Lady, Gawain becomes aware of the castle as it shimmers and shines through the white oaks (l. 772: "As hit schemered & schon þurȝ þe schyre okeȝ"). As he sits on his horse waiting on the bank of the deep, double-channeled ditch for the drawbridge to be lowered (ll. 785-86), he admires the beauty of the castle with its many chalk-white chimneys perched on the gleaming white tower roofs (ll. 798-99: "Chalk-whyt chymnees þer ches he in-noȝe,/Vpon bastel roueȝ þat blenked ful quyte").

If this predominance of white be intentional, it seems that the castle is meant to symbolize the house of the test of chastity and perhaps of Gawain's victory. It may be objected that the Lady's actions in her own home are hardly conducive to chastity. But we must remember that she is the instrument used to test Gawain's chastity and that there can be no virtue worth the name without temptation, or a victory without a test. The castle, where Gawain is victorious and where his virtue of chastity is proved, thus represents the house of the test of chastity and of the double victory—that of the spirit over the body and that of the ideals of knighthood over those of degenerate courtly love.

A weighty clue that color is used symbolically here is the explicit but purposely vague mention of other colors in referring to the painted pinnacles scattered everywhere among the embrasures of the castle.

So mony pynakle payntet watȝ poudred ay-quere
Among þe castle carneleȝ, clambred so þik
Þat pared out of papure purely hit semed. (ll. 800-02)

The Gawain-poet wishes merely to emphasize the whiteness of the castle in order to symbolize the test of chastity and omits the mention of other colors, lest he obscure the symbolism of the castle.

The Host

Gawain soon enters the castle and meets the Lord, whom we shall call the Host in succeeding pages. All we learn about his appearance is that he is a big man; his beard is broad, bright and beaver-colored; and his face is as fierce as fire.

Brode, bryȝt watȝ his berde, & al beuer-hwed,
. . . .
Felle face as þe fyre. . . . (ll. 845, 847)

Not once are his clothes or their color mentioned; nor is it necessary that they should be, for the medieval person would immediately characterize the Host from his reddish-brown beard and fiery red face. Curry says that red hair "in connection with red skin and beard is to be held in suspicion."[54] The strongest confirmatory evidence for this statement is the window of Chartres Cathedral, where reddish-black or brown or tan colors are associated with the hair and beard of Judas, with the devil, and with Jesus in the temptation scenes, to symbolize evil and sin, and temptation to these two. It is, therefore, highly probable that the reddish-brown beard and the red face symbolize the Host's position; it is he who causes his wife to tempt Gawain, his guest. The brown beard may symbolize the temptation to evil, the red face temptation to the particular evil of adultery.

Bedroom Colors

The Host commands Gawain to be brought to his bedroom. The bed is immediately described, for it is to figure prominently in the Temptations. The curtains about the bed have bright gold borders and are upheld by ropes running through red-gold rings,[55] while the coverlets are embroidered at the sides with white fur (ll. 854-57). The bedroom colors are thus red, gold, and white, the first two, the colors of Gawain's shield, the last that of the lining of his hood and of the diamonds about his head. Note that the colors of the bedroom are those of the principal actors in the temptation role—the red and gold of Gawain, the red and white (as we shall see) of the Lady. In the language of symbolism, the red signifies the love of the Lady as she sits on his bed, her frank invitation to the sin of adultery, and the courage Gawain will need to resist her; the gold signifies Gawain's integrity and his real worth proved true in the fires of temptation; and the white, Gawain's chastity and victory. Note how colors again predict the action of the poem.

It is interesting to observe that rich tapestries of Tuly and Tars hang on the walls, as they hung about Guenever in Arthur's halls. This similarity associates Gawain's test with Guenever and the sin imputed to her. And if the translation, *red silk of Toulouse*[56] for *of Tuly* (l. 858) be allowed, then the predominance of red would be a convincing indication for the symbolic meanings of love and adultery.

[54] Curry, *op. cit.*, pp. 18-19.

[55] According to *NED*, red gold was gold alloyed with copper. Curry cites an authority to the effect that the gold of the middle ages "was often darker than that of our own, and contained a considerable alloy of copper." Curry, *op. cit.*, p. 17.

[56] See *The College Survey of English Literature*, ed. by B. J. Whiting, and others (New York: Harcourt, Brace and Company, 1942), I, 122.

Gawain's Clothing

In his room, Gawain chooses a robe of brilliant colors so that by his appearance spring seems nigh (ll. 864-68). But in the great hall before the fireplace and in the presence of the knights at table Gawain is given a brown mantle (ll. 878-79). The failure to mention definite colors in the first robe he puts on and the specific mention of brown in the mantle (note that the mantle is something extra given to him) are significant facts which point to a special functional meaning of brown. Brown may foreshadow symbolically that Gawain, now in the house of the test of chastity, is to undergo temptation and that, needing self-restraint, he must begin to prepare himself by penance and humility. We have seen that brown often took its symbolism from the fact that it is the predominant color of the humble peasant class and was frequently used in the habits of monks. And it is no coincidence that Gawain's brown mantle and hood, like the hood of the Green Knight and the coat Gawain wears as he leaves Camelot, are lined with white, or ermine (ll. 878-81). The symbolism again indicates Gawain's basic purity and foreshadows his subsequent victory. The *pure white* table cloth on which the *fast*-day meal is taken may symbolize that the penance of the fast-day meal is necessary for *chastity*. Gawain follows his meal by devotions in chapel, prayer being the other traditional safeguard for temptations against chastity.

The Lady

After the meal and the devout Christmas Eve vespers in Chapel, Gawain hastens to salute the Host's wife. The Lady is pictured as having all the conventional attributes of the beautiful woman of the Middle Ages; she is the fairest of all others in skin, flesh, and face, and in her figure and her color (ll. 943-45). Rich red appears everywhere on her, contrasted with the brilliant white of her breast and naked throat and of the pearls she wears.

> Kerchofes of þat on wyth mony cler perle3,
> Hir brest & hir bry3t þrote bare displayed,
> Schon schyrer þen snawe þat schede[3] on hille3; . . . (ll. 954-56)

The fact that she is described in the traditional terms of the faultlessly beautiful woman of the romances is significant. It serves to associate her with the code of courtly love; for in the literature which exalted this code, the deified woman, despite her coldness and cruelty, was always portrayed by her troubadour lovers as possessing the conventional qualities of medieval beauty in a superlative degree.

Though the predominant red and white of her complexion are
conventional colors of feminine beauty, they are also highly symbolic.
The red signifies the Lady's amorous intent and boldness in bursting
into Gawain's room and, almost by force, tempting him to adultery;[57]
and her extreme whiteness reveals her true self—she herself is pure and
chaste; she is only the instrument of a test. The fact that the Gawain-
poet stresses the whiteness—whiter than the snow that falls on hills—
probably indicates his desire that we recognize her basic chastity. And
certainly, the fact that he stresses the rich red of her face and the "purer
than snow" whiteness of her breast and naked throat signifies that he
wishes to impress his hearers with her extreme beauty and sex appeal,
in order to show the difficulty of the Temptation test and, therefore,
the consequent great glory of Gawain's triumph.

The pearls that adorn the Lady are another example of the use of
gem symbolism. Since this is the first appearance of the Lady, we may
rightly expect the author to give us at this point a clue to her character
and to her particular function in the poem. Her pearls provide this
clue. In the New Testament pearls symbolize some valued personal
possession. Our Lord refers to the trader who sold all he had to buy the
pearl of great price (Heaven) [58] and warns His hearers not to cast
pearls before swine,[59] that is, not to expose one's most valued possession,
his chastity, to base creatures. The pearls the Lady wears in such
profusion symbolize that she is offering her pearl of great price, her
chastity, to Gawain—an offering she makes explicit in the first temptation. But it must be noted that, like the symbolism of her predominantly white complexion, the pearls signify that she is chaste and does
possess her pearl of great price.

Morgan le Fay

When Gawain went through the chancel to salute the Lady, he also
met the aged Morgan le Fay, who was leading the Lady by the hand.
That Morgan leads the Lady to Gawain is significant because it is
Morgan le Fay who has sent the Green Knight. Now she leads the
temptress to the tempted. Morgan is as ugly as the Lady is beautiful.
Her countenance is yellow, her rough wrinkled cheeks fall in loose
folds, her chin and eyebrows are black, her lips naked and bleared. She

---

[57] The predominant color assigned to Chaucer's sensuous, adulterous, and aggressive
Wife of Bath is red.
[58] Matt. 13: 45-46.
[59] Matt. 7: 6.

tries to conceal her forehead and chin in chalk-white veils (ll. 957-63). Her short and thick-set body and broad buttocks deprive her of any of the sex-appeal of the Lady (ll. 966-67).

The symbolism of the only two colors, yellow and black, which are used to describe Morgan le Fay,[60] is obvious and presents no difficulty. A dirty, or a pale, yellow symbolized treachery and deception in the Middle Ages, being the color of criminals and of Judas. Secondarily, it signifies jealousy and adultery. These meanings are very significant for a fuller understanding of the poem. The medieval listener would have immediately recognized Morgan's traditional treachery against Arthur's court and would have feared for Gawain. And the same listener would recall the traditional jealousy between Guenever and Morgan so prominent in the early Lancelot romances.[61] It is reasonable to conclude that this single use of yellow in the poem characterizes Morgan as malicious and indicates that her purpose in devising the tests was malevolent.[62]

The symbolism of black further confirms this conclusion. Curry says that the tendency of the Middle Ages was "to paint everything evil, wicked, malicious, and ugly in black colors...."[63] It is not too much to say that all the symbolic meanings of black—evil, witch-craft, wickedness, death, the powers of darkness—brood about Morgan, for it was her malicious desire to cause Guenever's death by fright and to cause Gawain's death in the Challenge test (ll. 2456-62). She is probably the prime mover in the temptation tests, the Host merely carrying out her wishes when he commands his wife to tempt Gawain; for she apparently has a secret power over all in the house, as the Gawain-poet indicates when he notes that she seemed to be greatly honored by the knights of the castle (l. 949). The Gawain-poet represents her as turreted and tricked out with ornamental details (l. 960),

---

[60] Morgan le Fay was ever a fascinating but fearful character to the medieval person. According to Roger S. Loomis, "Morgain la Fee and the Celtic Goddesses," *Speculum,* XX (1945), 183, the medieval romancers exhibited "a variety of attitudes, from extreme repugnance, to charmed wonder.... in their description of her person and the delineation of her character. Morgain may be the most beautiful of nine sister fays, or an ugly crone. She may be Arthur's tender nurse in the island Valley of Avilion, or his treacherous foe. She may be a virgin, or a Venus of lust."

[61] *Ibid.,* p. 186. Morgan ever tried to gain Lancelot's love and entice him to her by giving him magical qualities and powers in battle; but Lancelot ever rejected her advances because he is faithful to Guenever. Morgan was naturally jealous of Guenever's power to hold Lancelot's love.

[62] See pp. 82-83 of this study for a discussion of the opinion of Kittredge and Hulbert about the inclusion of Morgan in this poem.

[63] Curry, *op. cit.,* p. 88.

and the fact that she hides her black colors symbolically emphasizes her deceitfulness. It is significant that black is used only twice in the whole poem and both times with reference to her. She is definitely the sinister character in the poem.

Part Three—The Temptations

Introduction

The third part of the poem is devoted exclusively to the temptations and their parallels, the three hunting scenes. Restraint in the use of color in this section is noteworthy; in fact, colors occur less frequently here than in any of the other three parts. Thus, for example, when the Lady departs after each temptation and Gawain rises and dresses, there is no mention of color in his clothes. And the color of the Host's clothes receives no attention when he returns each evening. The only colors used in the Hunting scenes are the gray of the three greyhounds which rush at the fox (l. 1714), the white grease of the slain deer, the white tusks of the boar, and the brown hides (l. 1162) of the deer. Only the last mentioned color would seem to be used symbolically. Brown and reddish-brown, the colors (unexpressed but implied in the poem) of the deer, boar, and fox, are the predominant colors of the Hunting scenes. Because of the close parallel between the Temptation and Hunting scenes, not only the characteristics of the beasts, but also their colors may be related to the Temptation scenes. We have seen that brown and reddish-brown are the temptation colors; it may therefore be concluded that these colors serve as background tone during the Hunts to recall by suggestion the need Gawain has of humility and penance if he is to be victorious.

The Temptations

In the first temptation, the Lady is in her role of the typical medieval beauty; hence her lips are "small and laughing," and in her chin and "sweet cheek" red and white are mingled (ll. 1204-07). She is immediately recognized in her distinctive colors, red and white, which again symbolize her amorous external behavior but the purity of her true interior self. In the second temptation Gawain is mentioned as lying in bed, in clothes rich in color (l. 1471); but this vague reference is the only hint of color in the whole second test. The third temptation, however, is richest in symbolism, for here Gawain is hardest pressed to preserve his chastity. This temptation is definitely the deciding test; the Host realizes it, for in renewing the compact, he says that he has found Gawain trustworthy in two tests, and now "third time, turn out best."

For I haf fraysted þe twys & faythful I fynde þe,
Now þrid tyme, þrowe best, þenk on þe morne (ll. 1679-80).

The Lady realizes it, for she makes herself as seductive as possible, clothing herself in a pretty mantle reaching to the ground, clustering jewels in her hair, leaving her face and throat bare, and her breast naked (ll. 1736-41). Finally, Gawain realizes it, for he begs God to keep him from sin. And even Nature reflects the great test being enacted in the chamber—the sun rises fiery red. This emphasis on the color of the sun is significant, coming as it does, on the day of the third test. It symbolizes the great danger in which Gawain finds himself, the danger of passion and love running wild and resulting in the sin of adultery.

But Mary preserves her knight, and the lady acknowledges her defeat by asking for some keepsake. When Gawain courteously refuses to give her any, she offers him a ring of red gold—the ring, a symbol of betrothal, and the red symbolizing her feigned love for him. This, as the offers of her body and her love, is rejected. She then suddenly unknots her girdle and gives it to him. It is made of green silk and hemmed with gold (l. 1832). Gawain, of course, refuses such an obvious symbol of her self-surrender; but when he learns its magic properties, he weakens and for "love of his life" accepts it. The green and gold are the colors of the Green Knight and therefore of the Challenge. The Challenge is here united symbolically through color to the Temptation. The primary and most immediately recognizable symbolic meanings of the green in the girdle are the preternatural and life, for the girdle is a *magic* talisman which, in warding off death and wounds, is the promised means of preserving Gawain's *life*. In Gawain's possession, however, the girdle's green color secondarily symbolizes the chastity test just undergone and Gawain's victory. The gold hemming of the girdle symbolizes its value to Gawain and his own personal integrity and worth, now proven.

The Climax

When the Host returns from the hunt and enters the great hall, he finds Gawain wearing a blue mantle and a surcoat and hood, both adorned with white fur (ll. 1928-31). The white fur indicates again the basic spotlessness and purity of Gawain's character; but the emphasis here is on the blue mantle. This is the only time blue occurs in the poem; this fact, besides the rarity and preciousness of blue and the exalted position the color had in the Middle Ages, suggests that blue has here been reserved for a very special use. Gawain has just conquered in his most difficult and important test—the three temptations. He has proven his chastity and his fidelity to God, to Mary, and to the Host; he has vindicated the honor and fame of Arthur's court; he has shown himself to be the flower of true knighthood and the model of true chivalrous virtues. Consequently, he appears, in public and before the Host, wearing blue—the most spiritual of all colors next to white and the color of most exalted symbolic meanings. For blue, according to its use in the windows of Chartres Cathedral, in medieval German love poems, and in heraldry, symbolizes truth, fidelity, and loyalty, self-control and constancy, heavenly love and contemplation. Gawain has been faithful, the spirit has conquered over the flesh. This is truly the climax of the poem; and the language of color symbolism verifies and strengthens this conclusion.

A further indication that this is the climax of the poem is the fact that a mantle, as a piece of clothing, is used only twice in the entire poem, and in both these instances its color is emphasized. Before the Temptations Gawain wears a brown mantle to suggest his need for humility and penance; after the Temptations he wears a blue mantle to symbolize his utter faithfulness.

It is interesting to note that the mantle reaches to the earth, that is, it completely covers Gawain, symbolizing his total fidelity in chastity; and that the blue is worn in public before the Host to indicate to him personally Gawain's fidelity under his wife's temptations. It is also interesting to note that the white fur is no longer a lining, but that it is worn on the outside as an adornment (l. 1931: "Blande al of blaunner were boþe al aboute"), for now his basic purity and innocence have been made manifest externally.

Part Four—The Green Chapel

Gawain's Arming

The New Year comes in with wild snow storms, and the sleepless Gawain, hearing the shrill-blowing wind, rises before dawn and dresses. The richness and beauty of his clothing is stressed; he puts on the "loveliest" clothes; the usual fur linings and abundance of precious stones are in evidence; and for the first time his coat is velvet, a fabric which was very expensive in the Gawain-poet's time and which was the distinctive mark of nobility.[64] Gawain wraps the green silk girdle about his waist, and the poet calls attention to the striking effect of the gay green silk upon the rich red cloth.

Þe gordel of þe grene silke þat gay wel bisemed
Vpon þat ryol red cloþe þat ryche watȝ to schewe. (ll. 2035-36)

Thus we learn that his coat was red. The glittering gold border of the lace completes the triad of colors with which Gawain sets out for the Chapel: red, gold, green.

Since Gawain is arming for the adventure of the Green Chapel, the colors he wears take much of their symbolism from this coming event. Thus, the red coat[65] worn under his armor symbolizes primarily the courageous nature of the knight who goes so valiantly and purposefully to his adventure, and secondarily the blood that he will shed. The green of the girdle again symbolizes the *preternatural* qualities of the girdle in which his *hope* of saving his *life* is founded. The fact, however, that Gawain wears the girdle around his waist gives an added meaning to its green and gold colors.[66] The green now symbolizes that Gawain's *chastity* has been tested and proved, and the gold signifies that his *integrity* has likewise been tested in the refining fires of temptation and proved to be of great value and most glorious. Thus girt about his loins with the emblem of his personal chastity and integrity, he can confidently entrust himself to God. He puts his brilliant red and gold shield to his shoulder, spurs Gringolet with his gilded heels, and rides fearlessly across the bridge out toward the Chapel.

The Green Chapel

Before reaching the Green Chapel, Gawain rides through rough and barren country where mists envelope the hills, where brooks boil and foam along their banks, where steep banks and knobbed crags and jutting rocks and snow lying all about harmonize with the rough, bare branches of the trees. The only colors are grays and whites which intensify the bleakness and silence of the journey to the Chapel. This

[64] See Isobel D. Thornley, *England Under the Yorkists* (London: Longmans, Green and Co., 1920), p. 230. A sumptuary law passed in 1463 (but renewing "diverse ordinaries and statutes" made in past times), called attention to the "impoverishing of this realm of England," and decreed that "no esquire, nor gentleman, nor none under the degree of a knight ... shall wear ... any velvet, satin branched ... or any fur of ermine."

[65] It is interesting to note that this is the first time a coat (and not a mantle or hood) of Gawain is given a color.

[66] The green and gold, being the colors of the Green Knight, and therefore of the challenge, also look ahead to the event at the Green Chapel.

fearful journey is the last obstacle Gawain must overcome before meeting the Knight.

Arrived at the Chapel, Gawain finds it as terrible as the country through which he has ridden. In answer to his brave cry, the Green Knight appears, totally green as before at Camelot. Gawain bends his neck, and on the third blow, the blood from his slight wound gleams on the snow. When he realizes his deception in concealing the girdle from the Host, Gawain blushes red for shame at his fault, hurls the girdle at the Host; but, being pressed to take it, accepts it as a token of his shame, and rides away.

The use of color is interesting in this scene. Green predominates; it occurs eleven times—almost twice as often as all the other colors combined, for this is primarily the story of *life* at stake, of the *preternatural*, of *chastity*, and of the *hope* and *trust* of one man in God and in Mary, His Mother, to preserve him; red occurs three times, gold twice, and white once, for courage, integrity, and purity are the great factors determining Gawain's success. In these four colors the three main characters are represented here at the final scene; the Lady through her red and white, Gawain in his red and gold, and the Knight in his green and gold. Gawain and the Knight are physically present; but the Lady is also present by her influence, for it was her wooing and her girdle that caused the slight wound of the third stroke. This fact is symbolized by the explicit mention of the blood gleaming on the white snow. Red and white are the Lady's colors; the blood on the snow is the Lady's handiwork. This symbolic interpretation of Gawain's blood on the snow, fantastic though it may appear, is justifiable in a poem in which color symbolism has apparently been used with such consistency and artistry.

Arthur's Court

At Camelot, Gawain again blushes red for shame when he tells his adventures at the castle and the Green Chapel; but the court sees no cause for shame and agrees that each lord and lady of the Round Table shall wear a slantwise band of bright green for Gawain's sake (ll. 2513-21). The fact that Arthur's court wears a green baldric constitutes the concluding symbolism of the poem. The Gawain-poet explicitly states that the green silk baldric is the sign of the glory of the Round Table and the everlasting honor of any knight wearing it.

> For þat watȝ acorded þe renoun of þe Rounde Table,
> & he honoured þat hit hade, euer-more after, . . . (ll. 2519-20)

The baldric is the glory of the Round Table because it recalls the glorious adventure of its most illustrious representative. The green color of the baldric interprets the precise nature of the adventure. It is a *preternatural* adventure in which *chastity* has been tested and proved and *life* thereby saved; and it is an example of the courageous *hope* of the best of knights in God and Mary that they would preserve him. And the fact that the girdle, a traditional symbol of self-restraint, is now worn externally over the heart in the position of honor by each member of the court, symbolically indicates that the court has been tested in Gawain's adventure and has been found spotless in all knightly qualities but particularly in chastity. Finally, it is the everlasting honor of whoever wears it because it symbolizes that he, as a member of the noble court of Arthur, has been found true in chastity and all knightly qualities, owing to the adventure of that court's most illustrious Knight.

Heraldry, precious stones, Church liturgy, stained-glass windows, paintings, and literature—all provide evidence that there was a widespread use of color symbolism in the Middle Ages and that there was a particular code of color symbolism by which the individual colors had definite meanings attached to them.

As this study has attempted to show, the conscious use of a similar color symbolism by the Gawain-poet is clearly suggested. Thus, *Sir Gawain and the Green Knight* reveals a striking consistency in the use of certain colors with traditionally symbolic meanings and an equally striking appropriateness of these symbolic meanings to the interpretation of the basic meaning of the poem. Thus, again, an analysis and interpretation of the text reveals that the basic meaning of the poem is expressed on two different levels, one literal, the other satiric. The first meaning was found to be a test of Arthur's court, in the person of its most illustrious Knight, Sir Gawain, in all its knightly virtues and especially its chastity; the second meaning appears to be a satire of contemporary romances in their glorification of the code of courtly love (with its adulterous love, its deification of women, and its absurd sentimentality and artificiality), and in their glorification of a degenerate concept of chivalry.

Once the medieval color meanings and the double meaning of the poem are accepted, three things become evident—that the traditional color meanings can be attached to the colors used in the poem; that they harmonize with the interpretation of the poem; and that, in several striking instances, they give it a more unified, more conclusive, and richer meaning.

Perhaps chief in significance is the realization that color symbolism makes possible a clearer understanding of the basic meaning of the poem. For example, Professor Hulbert believes that *Sir Gawain and the Green Knight* is primarily a test of loyalty.[67] But a careful study of the use of color symbolism in the poem suggests that the poem is basically a chastity test. First, green is the predominant color in the poem. Obviously, it is the color of the preternatural Knight; but one of its medieval meanings is also chastity. And the fact that the girdle (which is a traditional symbol for continence, and which is given to Gawain *after* he has been victorious in the chastity test) is green further suggests the meaning of chastity. Again, it is Gawain's victory in the chastity test, symbolized by the green girdle, that saves his life at the Chapel and that suggests the chastity test as the essential test of the poem. Furthermore, the fact that blue, the most exalted and spiritual of colors, is used only once in the poem, and this directly after the three chastity tests, suggests that its use is very special and climactic. Thus, the blue robe which Gawain wears when he greets the Host on the evening of the third and last test symbolizes his constancy and fidelity to his ideals and to Mary, the chaste Virgin; but constancy and fidelity can only have meaning if they refer to his victory in the chastity tests, for he is unfaithful to his Host in concealing the gift of the girdle. Accordingly, the peculiar position of blue and its climactic use in the poem, as well as the greenness of the girdle suggest by color symbolism that the chastity test is the most important test of the poem.

Another example of how color symbolism clarifies the theme of the poem is provided by Morgan le Fay. Kittredge believes that Morgan was inserted into the poem by the Gawain-poet in order to "attach his narrative to the orthodox Arthurian narrative."[68] Kittredge's reason for this belief is that the Morgan plot is unconvincing:

---

[67] Hulbert, *op. cit.*, p. 694.

[68] Kittredge, *op. cit.*, p. 132.

... it is not worked into the fabric of the story; Fay's trick is a failure, there is no indication, in the author's description of the scene at court, that Guenever showed any particular alarm—certainly she was in no danger from shock. Besides one is rather surprised that Gawain should part with Bernlak on such cordial terms after the blunt avowal of his evil errand.[69]

And Professor Hulbert concurs with this belief that the Morgan plot was added by some "late redactor." He sees an "element of feebleness and inconsistency in the explanation of the test given by the Green Knight at the end."[70] His objection is that

... by it Gawain gains only greater glory, and Arthur's court a better reputation. Being an enchantress, she of course knew what would be the outcome of her scheme. ... What was her motive? What could she gain by the test?[71]

This study does not pretend to answer these arguments;[72] it merely suggests how an understanding of color symbolism indicates that Morgan has a definite organic place in the poem and that she is not attached merely to make the poem more Arthurian. The fact is that the only colors given her, black and yellow, would immediately identify her for the medieval listener as a malicious person—the black symbolizing witchcraft and evil; the yellow symbolizing treachery and jealousy. Hence her motive in sending the Green Knight to Camelot is jealousy of and hatred against Guenever and, therefore, against the whole court of Arthur. And that she really means to test them primarily for chastity is indicated by the single descriptive detail given to Guenever in the entire poem—gray eyes. Gray signifies innocence accused; and the eyes, the most revealing part of the body, would best express her character. Now it can only be Guenever's chastity that is being tested, because, in all the earlier romances, she was presented as having adulterous relations with Lancelot as well as with some of the other knights of the Round Table. Thus, the Morgan-theme is an integral part of the poem, for she it is who provides the motive of the test and sets in action the machinery of the whole poem.

Color symbolism also confirms our conclusion that the whole court is being tested particularly for chastity. The fact that Guenever, the

---

[69] *Ibid.*, pp. 132-133.

[70] Hulbert, *op. cit.*, p. 454.

[71] *Loc. cit.*

[72] It may be stated, however, against Hulbert that the magic properties of an enchantress did not always include knowledge of the future; and against Kittredge that Arthur does tell the Queen not to be dismayed over the strange occurrence of the Green Knight (l. 470).

Queen of the court, is accused for failures in chastity, indicates that the whole court is also suspect. And that the court adopts Gawain's green girdle, the emblem of his victory in chastity, suggests that it likewise has been tested for chastity in the person of Gawain.

Color symbolism thus further reinforces the first level of meaning of the poem; it does not, however, figure so prominently in the second level of meaning, for the implied satire is carried more in the conversations of the Lady and the Knight. However, color symbolisms do intensify this satire in that they suggest the ideal of chastity and knighthood. Thus Gawain's colors are gold and red on his shield to signify integrity and personal worth as well as courage. And since the Lady represents the norms of courtly love and degenerate chivalry, and Gawain the norm of chastity and true knighthood, the gold of his integrity and the red of his courage satirize the absence of these two qualities in that which is satirized. Moreover, the blue cloak he wears represents his constancy and fidelity, two virtues to which the courtly lovers of the romances could lay no claim so far as chastity was concerned. Thus Gawain, the ideal knight of the poem, is given only noble colors: red, gold, green.

It is thus clear that the code of color symbolism reinforces the basic meaning of the poem and in some instances makes it more clear and conclusive. But a close scrutiny of the color symbolism in this poem also reveals the misinterpretations into which a scholar may fall if he neglects obvious color meanings. Professor Hulbert appears to be guilty of two such misinterpretations when he states that "I do not think the pentangle has any great importance for the understanding of the fundamental story of *Gawain and the Green Knight*,"[73] and that the green lace is "obviously green because the Green Knight is green."[74] Besides the pentangle itself, which symbolizes Gawain's virtues and indicates what he is being tested for, the red and gold colors tell us, in the language of heraldry, of his courage as well as of his great personal worth and nobility—he is the ideal of *true* knighthood arming for the test of his

---

[73] Hulbert, *op. cit.*, p. 730. See, *ibid.*, p. 721: "It [the pentangle] constitutes, in fact, practically the only digression in the poem."

[74] *Ibid.*, p. 709. Hulbert goes so far as to say, *ibid.*, p. 710: "Were it not for the fact that the green insisted on in this poem has a meaning ['The Knight wears green because he is an Other-World creature . . . ,' p. 709], one might suppose that green was merely a code word for another color, and that the initiate might supply for it blue . . . or some other color."

purity and for his *true* knightly virtue of courage. The greenness of the girdle, it is true, reminds us of the preternatural Green Knight and his Challenge, but it almost certainly is an emblem also of Gawain's chastity.

A further use of color symbolism in *Sir Gawain and the Green Knight* is similar to that of the themes and motifs in a symphony; colors serve to identify the principal characters and to plot the action of the entire poem.

The suiting of colors to the characters reveals the Gawain-poet's artistry. Thus the noble Gawain's colors are red and gold; the evil Morgan's are black and yellow; the Green Knight's green and gold; the Lady's red and white; the Host's brown; and Guenever's gray. The action of the poem can likewise be charted by means of colors. Green, by far the most prevalent color, indicates the preternatural element in the poem. Though the Green Knight early disappears, not to reappear till the very end, the constant recurrence of the color green, as an undertone throughout the poem, will not let us forget Gawain's strange quest for the Green Chapel and his *hope* of saving his *life* there. The brave Gawain who accepts the Green Knight's challenge is recognized by his red and gold, colors which signify the courage and the integrity needed both to persevere in his quest for the Green Chapel and to preserve his chastity. He comes to the house of the test of chastity, recognized as such by its shimmering white. The first opposing force he meets there is the Lady, whose red colors indicate that she is the passionate and love-compelling force. Her predominantly white colors, however, suggest that she is non-malicious and innocent in her intentions, a fact we learn at the Chapel when Bercilak tells Gawain that he commanded his wife to tempt Gawain (ll. 2360-61). The second opposing force is Morgan le Fay, whose black and yellow colors immediately identify her as the only totally evil and malicious character and the one who devised both the test and its obstacles. The brown color of the Host suggests the Temptations he has commanded his wife to employ. And Gawain, for his first appearance in the great hall, is given a brown mantle, a fact suggesting his need of penance to gain spiritual strength for the Temptations he is about to undergo; the blue mantle he wears after the three temptations signifies his glorious fidelity and loyalty to his knightly ideal of chastity. Finally, the green in the girdle, which he receives from the Lady at the third temptation, takes on the added meaning of chastity and identifies Gawain's chastity test with his preternatural adventure at the Green Chapel. As worn by all members of Arthur's court, the green is the perpetual symbol of Gawain's twofold victory— in the chastity test and in his faithful fulfillment of the conditions of the Challenge.

Thus, like the themes of a symphony, the dominant colors rise high and then fade away, appear and disappear and reappear again, one played off against the other until the poem closes in a grand finale with the chastity victory symbolized by the blue cloak and the memory of the twofold victory perpetuated by the symbolically green baldric.

CPSIA information can be obtained at www.ICGtesting.com
Printed in the USA
BVOW06s1716270116

434482BV00017B/69/P

9 781163 133811